T0311560

The Future of Auditing

The Future of Auditing provides a concise overview of the function of auditing and the future challenges it faces, underpinned with suggestions for future research. It evaluates the key challenges facing the profession, such as quality, competition, and governance, as well as highlighting the under-explored areas of ethics, fraud, and judgement. The emphasis throughout is on the value of audit, and the importance of auditing research.

Providing an original assessment of global versus national auditing, evidence-based auditing standards, and the structure of professional firms, David Hay critically examines the value of auditing from different standpoints. He critically reviews current assumptions about the value of audits of financial statements, and explores research opportunities and priorities to improve understanding of the value of auditing and its future role and function.

This authoritative but accessible guide to the future of auditing and the challenges it faces will be useful not only to auditing researchers, but also to policy makers, standard setters, financial journalists, and auditing professionals seeking an accessible overview of current and future issues in auditing.

David Hay is Professor of Auditing at the University of Auckland, New Zealand. He was previously Head of the Department of Accounting and Finance at the University of Auckland. He has been an external reviewer of accounting degree programs at more than ten universities and similar institutions in New Zealand, Australia, Malaysia, and Hong Kong. David and his co-authors won the 2017 "Notable Contribution to the Auditing Literature Award" presented by the Auditing Section of the American Accounting Association.

Routledge Focus on Accounting and Auditing

Advances in the fields of accounting and auditing as areas of research and education, alongside shifts in the global economy present a constantly shifting environment. This presents challenges for scholars and practitioners trying to keep up with the latest important insights in both theory and professional practice. *Routledge Focus on Accounting and Auditing* presents concise texts on key topics in the world of accounting research.

Individually, each title in the series provides coverage of a key topic in accounting and auditing, whilst collectively, the series forms a comprehensive collection across the discipline of accounting.

The Boundaries in Financial and Non-Financial Reporting
A Comparative Analysis of their Constitutive Role
Laura Girella

The Future of Auditing
David Hay

For more information about the series, please visit www.routledge.com/
Routledge-Focus-on-Accounting-and-Auditing/book-series/RFAA

The Future of Auditing

David Hay

Routledge
Taylor & Francis Group

LONDON AND NEW YORK

First published 2020
by Routledge
2 Park Square, Milton Park, Abingdon, Oxon OX14 4RN

and by Routledge
605 Third Avenue, New York, NY 10017

First issued in paperback 2021

Routledge is an imprint of the Taylor & Francis Group, an informa business

Publisher's Note
The publisher has gone to great lengths to ensure the quality of this
reprint but points out that some imperfections in the original copies may
be apparent.

British Library Cataloguing-in-Publication Data
A catalogue record for this book is available from the British Library

Library of Congress Cataloging-in-Publication Data
Names: Hay, David, 1955– author.
Title: The future of auditing / by David Hay.
Description: New York, NY : Routledge, 2019. | Series: Routledge focus
    on accounting and auditing
Identifiers: LCCN 2019015269 | ISBN 9781138477087 (hardback : alk.
    paper) | ISBN 9781351105484 (ebook)
Subjects: LCSH: Auditing.
Classification: LCC HF5667 .H3648 2019 | DDC 657/.45—dc23
LC record available at https://lccn.loc.gov/2019015269

ISBN 13: 978-1-03-209193-8 (pbk)
ISBN 13: 978-1-138-47708-7 (hbk)

Typeset in Times New Roman
by Apex CoVantage, LLC

Contents

Acknowledgements   vi

1   Overview: the future of auditing   1

2   The value of auditing   3

3   The future of auditing   25

4   Opportunities for auditing research   50

Index   65

Acknowledgements

I appreciate the invaluable comments and advice provided by Robert Knechel and Marleen Willekens, and the excellent work by the authors of each chapter in *The Routledge Companion to Auditing.*

1 Overview

The future of auditing

Financial statement auditing is important because financial reporting misstatements are dangerous. They can lead investors to make bad decisions, cause lenders to take unnecessary risks, and reward managers when they do not deserve to be rewarded. Poor quality accounting and auditing can be bad for a whole country's economy.

A general definition of auditing is that it is an assurance service which improves the quality of information or its context. In the context of financial statement auditing, which is the type of auditing that I mainly address in this book, financial reporting information is "better" – more credible, more reliable – because an auditor has examined evidence about the assertions making up the financial statements and convinced management to make changes that improve the accuracy and informativeness of financial statements. The assurance provided by an auditor allows financial statement users to better rely on the information. It has been vetted by an auditor whose conclusions are stated in the audit report.

Auditing has economic benefits, some of which are not always immediately obvious, for both the audited company and its management and the national (or global) economy as a whole. To understand auditing, it is necessary to be aware of those benefits.

The book examines the value of auditing, at present and in the future, from several perspectives. The perspectives include examining current understanding of why audits of financial statements are valuable; emerging issues that are important to the future of auditing; research opportunities about the understanding of the value of auditing; and research opportunities about the future of auditing.

Chapter 2 explains how auditing has value, using several different perspectives. Chapter 3 explores issues about its future and how it might change, and Chapter 4 examines research opportunities arising from Chapter 2 and Chapter 3. Chapter 2 and Chapter 4 further develop the material in Chapters 1 and 28 of *The Routledge Companion to Auditing*, "The function of auditing" and "The future of auditing research" (Hay et al., 2014a; Hay et al., 2014b). The extended format allows me to further develop the discussion of the reasons for auditing and allows for greater links between the theory and suggestions for future research. The new book expands discussion of current issues.

The value of an audit, and the future of auditing research, are topics that are fundamental to auditing. This book is intended to be useful to decision makers who are not familiar with the research in this area, including legislators, policy makers, news media experts, standard setters, and research students. This book provides a single source that will gives a background to these fundamental issues and a source of further references to expand from.

References

Hay, D. C., W. R. Knechel, and M. Willekens. 2014a. Introduction: The Function of Auditing. In *The Routledge Companion to Auditing*, edited by D. C. Hay, W. R. Knechel, and M. Willekens, 1–10. Abingdon, Oxford: Routledge.

———. 2014b. The Future of Auditing Research. In *The Routledge Companion to Auditing*, edited by D. C. Hay, W. R. Knechel, and M. Willekens, 351–357. Abingdon, Oxon, UK: Routledge.

2 The value of auditing

Audits are valuable to a surprising range of parties, and some of the explanations for the valuation of auditing are counter-intuitive.[1] We start with a simple explanation of the benefits of auditing provided by Willekens (2007), using the market for used cars as a parallel. Buying a used car is risky. Most car buyers are not experts, and cannot judge whether assertions made by the car salesman are reasonable and reliable. In the same way, shareholders and other stakeholders in a company are not able to find out whether assertions made by the directors are also reliable. In the case of the company, the assertions might be about how much profit the company has made or how liquid is its financial position. Assertions are made through the financial statements.

The used car buyer has the choice of not buying the car and taking the bus to work instead; or they could get an expert to investigate and give an opinion on the assertions made by the seller. To help the deal go through, the seller might even pay for a trustworthy expert to provide a report (e.g., a vehicle history report from CARFAX in the USA). In much the same way, potential investors have the option of not buying shares of a company if they are uncertain about the reliability of the accounts. Or they can rely on an auditor, as the expert on financial statement assertions, to give them a report on management-provided financial information. It might be in management's interests to engage a respected auditor if that helps investors to decide to commit their funds to the company.

The auditor does not give an opinion of the worth of the company or whether it is a wise investment. Rather, the audit report provides assurance that what management says is reliable.

The used car example is helpful up to a point, but auditing of financial statements takes place in a setting of much greater complexity. It is more complex than buying a used car because of the number of people involved and the ambiguity of financial information. If there are many shareholders and other stakeholders, it is not feasible to allow them all to examine the company's records in detail. There is also a wide range of parties involved in running the company – directors, audit committee members, management – all with their own self-interest, as well as their own views of what are the company's best interests. In addition, there is a well-known expectation gap, whereby different users have different ideas of what the auditor can do – compared to what the auditor intends or is able to do. The amounts involved may be very large, and the underlying financial and accounting issues can be very complex. In many cases, there are operations and stakeholders in a variety of different international jurisdictions. And finally, auditing is usually controlled by regulation and professional standards.

There are a number of economic explanations for auditing, and these explanations overlap. They all provide reasonable explanations as to why managers might find it to be in their interests to submit to an audit, which they do implicitly when taking a job in a company that undergoes an audit. In addition, in many cases, auditing is required by law. The regulation of auditing can be explained by legislators looking after the interests of stakeholders who may not be able to influence the decisions of a company directly. It can also be explained in terms of the interests of the legislators. The next section discusses fundamental theories underlying the benefits of auditing.

A Explanations for the value of auditing

Auditing can be seen as having an agency role; an information role; an insurance role; a management control role; a corporate governance role; and a confirmation role. These are the economic explanations for auditing. In all of these explanations, managers might voluntarily submit to being audited because it is in their own interests. In addition, in many settings auditing is compulsory – but the economic explanations for why auditing is desirable still apply, and companies may engage an auditor to carry out something more than the absolute minimum level of audit effort required by auditing standards. The reasons why auditing is often compulsory are also important in understanding the function of auditing, and explanations for compulsory auditing are discussed later.

1 The agency (or monitoring) explanation

Shareholders are aware that managers may act in their own interest, and could report misleading information as a result. Agency relationships apply where one party (the principal) delegates authority, especially control over resources, to another (the agent) (Wallace, 1980, 12–13). When agency relationships apply, there are agency costs. Agents might be self-interested and spend money for their own benefit, or might shirk their duties, or might be diligent but misguided. If nothing is done to avoid these possibilities, then the principal will be less inclined to enter into this relationship. The principal will spend less, or even avoid entering into the transactions altogether, reducing the scope of the agents' activities or putting them out of work entirely. Investors might discount the information they receive, and pay a lower price for shares than the financial fundamentals would justify if the financial reports could be trusted (if they can be persuaded to invest at all). Agents have the incentive to prevent that from happening by arranging to reduce the costs of monitoring. The agent might appoint an auditor to report on the financial statements in order to give the principal more confidence and reduce monitoring costs. It becomes worthwhile from a manager's point of view to provide auditing as a form of bonding of the manager, or monitoring on behalf of the shareholders. Agency costs include the costs that arise when otherwise useful activities are not undertaken because the risks are too high that the self-interested agent will take advantage of the situation, or when the principal expends effort in overseeing the agent.

Thus, audits exist because of "price protection." Price protection means that shareholders (or other stakeholders) might discount the information they receive, and pay a lower price for shares than the financial fundamentals would justify, because they know some managers in some situations might have an incentive to provide misleading information (Jensen and Meckling, 1976, 325; Pincus, Rusbarsky, and Wong, 1989, 243). In 1994, a senior partner in the US firm of KPMG wrote that "auditing adds tremendous value" (Elliott, 1994). Elliott estimates that audits reduce the cost of capital by 1% to 3%. Elliott estimated that a company without an audit might have to pay 1% to 3% more for capital, by which he meant that "for a company with $10 billion in capital, the comparable annual savings would be $100 million to $300 million!" (Elliott, 1994, 74). Empirical studies suggest that this effect is not as large as Elliott thought, although a substantial and statistically significant effect (0.25%) is present (Blackwell, Noland, and Winters, 1998). More evidence in support of each of the explanations is provided in the next section.

A price-protection explanation might apply when the managers of a company are applying for a loan – they can expect a better response, and perhaps a lower interest rate, if they can produce audited financial statements. Where auditing is compulsory, they can reduce agency costs by providing auditing of more than the minimum standard required (for example, an audit by a large accounting firm with an international reputation for high-quality audits). There is research supporting the argument that Big 4 audits are associated with lower cost of capital than non-Big 4 audits (Khurana and Raman, 2004, 488).

Historical evidence shows that audits were sometimes arranged voluntarily, as predicted by the agency explanation, before legislation made them mandatory (Wallace, 1980; Chow, 1982). Monitoring, bonding and other contracting explanations are supported by previous studies that provide evidence that auditing (or similar assurance services) is necessary when there would otherwise be high agency costs, indicated by greater size, higher debt leverage, or lower managerial ownership (Chow, 1982). Voluntary disclosure, voluntary auditing, and voluntary formation of audit committees are all associated with variables representing higher agency costs such as greater size, higher leverage, or lower managerial ownership (Salamon and Dhaliwal, 1980; Chow, 1982; Pincus et al., 1989). There is evidence that Big N audit firms, which are perceived to provide higher quality audits, are able to charge higher audit fees (Simunic, 2014, 36). This finding supports the argument that managers find higher quality audits valuable.

2 The information (or signaling) explanation

Better information leads to better, more informed decisions, by both managers and outsiders. Auditing can be a way both to improve information, and to demonstrate (or "signal") that it is better. Company managers have better information about the value and quality of the business that they run than do outside investors or stakeholders. But if managers make statements in the financial report that claim that their business is a better investment than others, their claims may not be believed. This imbalance in knowledge about a business is called "information asymmetry."

One way of overcoming this information asymmetry is for managers to engage an auditor to provide assurance about their statements. Appointing an auditor is then a signal to investors that they can place more credibility on the company's financial statements. Where auditing is compulsory, then managers can still provide a signal of higher quality by appointing an auditor of higher quality – perhaps a large international firm or a firm that is considered a specialist in the client's industry. This can be a means of signaling insiders' knowledge of superior performance and reduced measurement error (Wallace, 1987).

Managers can add credibility and increase the value of their business, for example in an initial public offering of shares (IPO), by engaging a higher quality auditor (Titman and Trueman, 1986). An entrepreneur who has more favorable private information about their firm will choose a higher quality auditor; investors are able to infer that the entrepreneur has favorable information from the choice of auditor, and entrepreneurs with less favorable private information are not able to mimic this signal (Titman and Trueman, 1986, 160). There is evidence that managers of IPOs use the choice of a nationally-known auditor to signal higher quality, and that this results in higher IPO returns (Beatty, 1989, 707).

3 The insurance (or "deep pockets") explanation

It is sometimes suggested that stakeholders may demand audits as a way of increasing the chance of recovering certain types of losses. The auditor provides a "target" that they might be able to take legal action against to recover any investment losses from, because the auditor has resources ("deep pockets") (Chow, 1982).

Providers of external financing and custodians of others' funds may demand audits as a way of increasing the chance of recovering certain types of losses (Chow, Kramer, and Wanda, 1988). The auditor is a "target" that they might be able to sue to recover any potential investment losses. Investors or lenders can sue those directly involved, including directors and management, but these people may not have the resources to make up the losses of investors. Auditors are seen as the "deep pockets" defendant (who will have greater funds available after the company has failed than most managers or directors individually) and, as a result, auditors can face costly litigation even when they have little or no responsibility for the losses. This view treats the audit something like a put option against future bad behavior or misleading reporting.

Evidence supporting the insurance hypothesis is reported in studies of the failure of audit firm Laventhol & Horwath. When a large second-tier firm went into bankruptcy, and therefore no longer provided insurance, its clients had adverse share price reactions (Menon and Williams, 1994; Baber, Kumar, and Verghese, 1995). This result was taken as evidence that the insurance hypothesis applies. A more recent study regarding events surrounding an investigation into KPMG by the US Department of Justice found a similar effect (Brown, Shu, Soo, and Trompeter, 2013).

The insurance explanation was influential in the development of the law of negligence in Commonwealth countries in the late twentieth century. Auditors were held to be liable to a larger number of third parties. Courts are now applying the law in a less expansive manner than earlier, and requiring evidence of reliance on the auditor's work (Pacini, Hillison, Alagiah, and Gunz, 2002). Auditors themselves tend to see the insurance model of auditing as unreasonable and unfair, but nevertheless evidence exists that stakeholders believe that it applies.

4 The management control explanation

Management control for the benefit of the internal management of the organization is another explanation for auditing, especially in smaller companies that may be family-owned or have less complex financial structures. Some business owners purchase voluntary audits as part of a control system within their organization.

Agency explanations do not apply to family businesses where there is no separation between ownership and control. In a small organization, the owner-manager controls operations by direct supervision and personal observation. As an organization grows larger, control becomes more difficult. Delegation becomes necessary, and there is a risk of moral hazard and that the subordinate managers who have delegated authority will act opportunistically. Abdel-khalik (1993) showed that private companies are more likely to voluntarily choose to have an audit when they have more layers of hierarchy or are larger. He argues that auditing helps top management to control complex organizations as a compensatory control system for organizational loss of control in hierarchical organizations. His evidence supports this explanation because there are significant relationships between audit fees and the number of layers of hierarchy and size.

5   The corporate governance explanation

Auditing is closely associated with corporate governance. Corporate governance is defined as the "system by which companies are directed and controlled."[2] It consists of the board of directors of a company, or their equivalent, and other mechanisms such as an audit committee, other board committees, and the external auditors. The elements of corporate governance vary around the world. For example, in some countries banks play a part (La Porta, Lopez-de-Silanes, Shleifer, and Vishny, 2000). It has been described as "mosaic" of different interactions among auditors and "other actors such as management, the audit committee, and the board of directors" (Cohen, Krishnamoorthy, and Wright, 2004, 780).

It is thus useful to see auditing as a complement to the other elements of corporate governance. As such, it is a critical element in an organization's risk management strategy. Auditing can be a useful way to reduce the risks faced by the stakeholders of a company, especially for organizations whose stakeholders are subject to higher risk (Knechel and Willekens, 2006). Other complementary mechanisms are also used to reduce risk, such as internal audits, audit committees and independent directors.

The interaction of these various mechanisms can have complex results, because the audit committee members and external directors become stakeholders themselves, and also seek to minimize risk, especially any risk that their reputations might be damaged. As a result, the demand for auditing, or for higher-quality auditing, can be greater when there are other governance mechanisms in place. Knechel and Willekens (2006) show that demand for external auditing, indicated by higher audit fees, increases in situations where there are multiple stakeholders. Because individual decisions about control processes and procedures may shift benefits and costs among groups of stakeholders, the net investment in auditing may increase when multiple stakeholders become involved in corporate governance decisions. Each stakeholder benefits from a greater level of control, while being able to shift a share of the costs to the other stakeholders. Knechel and Willekens (2006) found evidence that audit fees are higher when a company has an audit committee, discloses a relatively high level of financial risk management, and has a larger proportion of independent board members. Audit fees are lower when a company discloses a relatively high level of compliance risk management. These results are consistent with other studies.

Bédard and Compernolle (2014, 256–259) review research showing that stronger audit committees are associated with choosing higher quality auditors, greater control over the risk of non-audit services and increased negotiating power for auditors compared to managers. There is a tendency for governance to be enhanced in recent times, and this is usually associated with greater demand for auditing. Better corporate governance is thus not a substitute for auditing, but a complement.

6 The confirmation hypothesis

A further explanation is provided by the "confirmation" hypothesis. The confirmation hypothesis, examined by Ball, Jayaraman, and Shivakumar (2012), states that audited financial reporting and the disclosure of managers' private information are complementary. Announcements by companies, such as profit announcements, contain information that has mostly been reflected already in share prices. This finding by Ball and Brown (1968) has been well-documented. That paper, and others like it, appeared to leave little room for auditing to be of value to the financial markets – audited financial information arrives too late for it to be useful. As a result, audited announcements of financial information usually do not add as much information as announcements of new, price-sensitive information (Ball and Brown, 1968, 176). Under the confirmation hypothesis, announcements about past financial performance and position are still important, because they verify earlier unaudited announcements. Ball et al. (2012) suggest that "audited financial reporting and voluntary disclosure of managers' private information are complementary mechanisms for communicating with investors, not substitutes," and that "managers are encouraged to be more truthful when they are aware their disclosures of private information subsequently will be confirmed" (Ball et al., 2012, 136). This is the confirmation hypothesis. It suggests that while voluntary announcements of private information held by managers have market impact, they need to be backed up later by subsequent audited financial reports. Ball et al. (2012) also argue that the impact of unaudited announcements is greater when managers have committed more resources to independent audit by paying higher audit fees (Ball et al. 2012, 137).[3] Other research questions that examine the confirmation hypothesis can be suggested: for example, examining the impact of auditors on market reactions to unexpected announcements.

Ball et al. (2012) found evidence to support the confirmation hypothesis by showing that companies which make more frequent and more specific management forecast announcements also commit to greater auditing. Nevertheless, very little evidence to support the confirmation hypothesis has been provided as yet, and such evidence as exists is ambiguous. The confirmation hypothesis is plausible in understanding why auditing is important, even when unaudited announcements are widely used and unaudited information often has more impact.[4]

7 Other explanations

Other explanations from management literature are also sometimes useful in explaining how auditing is valuable, especially stakeholder theory, institutional theory (more precisely, neo-institutional theory), and legitimacy theory. These three theoretical models are related, and discussions often link them to each other (Deegan, 2014, 349). Under legitimacy theory, organizations undertake actions intended to increase their appearance of legitimacy to society as a whole (Gray, Kouhy, and Levers, 1995). Under stakeholder theory, they will make disclosures in response to the demands of their most influential stakeholders. Institutional theory explains that organizations will tend to become similar to each other as a result of three influences: namely, coercive, normative, and mimetic isomorphism (Gray et al., 1995; DiMaggio and Powell, 1983). Coercive isomorphism takes place through formal processes like regulation. Normative isomorphism occurs when managers and organizations follow socially constructed values that are created through education, especially among professionals. Mimetic isomorphism takes place when managers copy other entities (DiMaggio and Powell, 1983). These models are often used to explain additional disclosures such as corporate social responsibility reporting (Gray et al., 1995; Ortas, Álvarez, Jaussaud, and Garayar, 2015; Adnan, van Staden, and Hay, 2010). Organizations might also adopt similar auditing or corporate governance practices because of these three types of isomorphism. Baker, Bédard, and Prat dit Hauret (2014) apply institutional theory to explain why international developments in the regulation of auditing made national requirements for auditing standard setting and inspection of audit work become more similar across different countries in the period after the Sarbanes-Oxley Act (Baker et al., 2014). Heald (2018, 1) suggests that in some countries, institutional arrangements such as public sector settings are simply copied from previous colonial institutions, and constitute "mimetic isomorphism without recognition of context."

The "audit society" is a term used to show how auditing has become more influential in recent decades, and it is not generally used in a way that perceives auditors in a favorable light. Michael Power argues that there has been an "audit explosion" that permeates society, that in the United Kingdom was associated with Thatcherism, and that is detrimental to society (e.g., Power, 1994; Power, 2000). Although Power's model has been criticized, particularly because his work does not define what he means by "auditing" (Maltby, 2008), it has been influential to the extent of spreading beyond the auditing literature and into wider areas of social science (Shore and Wright, 2015). Social scientists like Shore and Wright (2015) portray auditing as a harmful influence.

B Evidence about the explanations for the value of auditing

Empirical evidence for or against these explanations for the value of auditing is not easy to come by, since auditing is so highly regulated in most settings. Nevertheless, evidence about the value of auditing has been explored in quite a few ways.

Even when auditing is mandatory, firms are free to choose which auditors they hire. There are many arguments suggesting that larger audit firms are of higher quality, especially the Big 4 international auditing firms (Deloitte, EY, KPMG, and PwC). These firms have more incentive to maintain high quality to protect their brand name, and more to lose if there is an audit failure. They also charge higher fees, which also suggests that their audits are more highly valued (Simunic, 1980). They have been less likely to suffer from lawsuits (Palmrose, 1988). Other studies have also considered whether audit firms specializing in a particular industry provide higher quality audits (Craswell, Francis, and Taylor, 1995; Francis, Reichelt, and Wang, 2005; Lawrence, Minutti-Meza, and Zhang, 2011; Audousset-Coulier, Jeny, and Jiang, 2016). The evidence about whether specialization has an impact on audit quality or fees is still rather mixed.

Research studies have shown that there are associations between companies choosing higher quality auditors and the incentives of the companies under the agency and signaling (information) explanations. For example, companies choosing larger (higher quality) auditors have less initial public offering (IPO) underpricing, and higher earnings response coefficients (defined as a larger stock market reaction to unexpected earnings announcements) (Beatty, 1989; Teoh and Wong, 1993). A study using historical data from a period before auditing was compulsory found that debt contracts were associated with engaging an independent auditor (Chow, 1982).

Further evidence about the agency and signaling explanations shows that audited firms pay lower interest rates than non-audited firms (Blackwell et al., 1998). Firms whose auditors confirm an increase or decrease in internal control effectiveness then experience a decrease or increase in cost of equity (Ashbaugh-Skaife, Collins, Kinnery, and LaFond, 2009, 1). Changes in auditing regulation that exempt some companies from an audit have been examined in some studies, which show that those companies that voluntarily continued to have an audit received an upgrade to their credit rating (Lennox and Pittman, 2011; Dedman and Kausar, 2012). Public sector evidence about the agency explanation is provided by Zimmerman (1977) and Baber (1983) and about agency and signaling by Evans and Patton (1987). The signaling explanation is applied to other settings in other recent studies (e.g., Hay and Davis, 2004; Gore, 2004).

There is further evidence about the signaling and insurance explanations (Willenborg, 1999; Mansi, Maxwell, and Miller, 2004). Willenborg (1999, 226) examines the demand for auditing in small initial public offerings, where the financial reports are less important but the insurance role of auditors is more important, and shows "particularly strong" support for the insurance explanation as well as for support for signaling. Mansi et al. (2004, 760) control for the influence of other sources of information to the bond market, and are able to show that auditors have both a signaling and an insurance role that is important.

Evidence for the management control role of auditing is mainly provided by Abdel-khalik (1993), which contains vivid anecdotal evidence as well as statistical evidence that there is a relationship between levels of hierarchy and voluntary auditing. Hay (2003) shows that there is a relation between auditing and decentralization in a public sector setting, also consistent with the management control explanation.

Evidence about the demand for auditing as part of governance is provided by studies showing that boards with better governance mechanisms also pay higher audit fees (Carcello, Hermanson, Neal, and Riley, 2002; Abbott, Parker, Peters, and Raghunandan, 2003). Srinidhi, He, and Firth (2014) show that family firms with stronger governance also demand more auditing.

The confirmation explanation (Ball et al., 2012) has not been widely explored. However, there is some further evidence. Şabac and Tian (2015) use an analytical model to show that "hard" information in audited financial statements can be useful in confirming "soft" information in management reports. Hay and Cordery (2018) suggest that this explanation could be applicable to government announcements and financial reports.

This set of explanations is overlapping but nevertheless contrasting. The explanations, as they have developed over recent decades, have also had a practical effect on how judges in lawsuits against auditors view the role of the auditor. Pacini et al. (2002) review the trend in auditors' liability in the United Kingdom, Canada, Australia, and New Zealand. They show that in the second half of the twentieth century, judges in cases involving auditors initially showed a trend towards an insurance explanation for auditing. They tended to increase the responsibility and liability placed on auditors, and allowed stakeholders with a relatively distant relationship with auditors to claim for losses. Later judgments moved more towards contracts-based monitoring views of auditing, and restricted liability to those contracting for the audit and to a very limited class of third parties.

The economic explanations for the value of auditing are relevant to understanding current issues because they portray auditing as something that is beneficial in itself, not a necessary evil that must be imposed by regulation. In discussing current issues, such as whether auditors should be required to report on internal control, or whether auditor rotation is beneficial, it is helpful to recall that auditing is fundamentally in the interests of a company and its managers and directors. Each of these explanations also tends to imply that demand for auditing arises naturally, since there are many reasons why companies would of their own accord choose auditors of a suitable quality. In addition, however, there are elements of auditing related to a "public good" that suggest that auditing should be regulated.

In practice, auditing is usually regulated, and there has been a tendency for it to become more and more regulated. The question is not whether regulation is needed but, rather, how much is needed. This includes standard setting. The economic explanations for auditing also help to explain why auditing has been a long-established part of doing business, and why its strong position has not been weakened by decades of auditing scandals and audit failures.

C Explanations for the regulation of auditing

The explanations discussed so far are very helpful in showing why auditing is demanded on a voluntary basis. It offers many advantages to investors and other stakeholders, as well as to managers. But in most cases where auditing is important, it is required by some form of regulation. To understand the value of auditing, we need to consider why in many settings auditing is compulsory, especially for listed companies.

According to the economic theory of regulation, there is a good reason for regulatory intervention when a free market solution would not work (which is called market failure). Market failures are usually caused by lack of adequate information, lack of competition, or by externalities, and exist when the quantity or quality of a good supplied differs from what would be best for society as a whole. In such cases, government regulation that moves the output of a good closer to what would be best for society can improve social welfare. Applied to the market for audited financial information, market failure exists if the output of audited information in annual reports or distributed via other corporate communication channels is non-optimal for stakeholders' decision making (Willekens, Steele, and Miltz, 1996; Eilifsen and Willekens, 2008; Langli and Willekens, 2018).

A related reason why audit demand is regulated is also that auditing is a kind of public good. That is, once an audit is produced, many stakeholders can benefit, even if they are not a party to hiring and compensating the auditor. Economic theory suggests that a public good will be produced at a less than ideal level unless some form of regulation is introduced. Since most stakeholders have little direct control over a company, there is a concern that too little auditing may be demanded, in spite of the natural demand of auditing as a risk management tool. Small shareholders, potential investors, and many other groups are perceived to benefit from an audit, but they cannot impose it on a company. For that reason, legislators impose auditing requirements for the benefit of the community.[5]

Many stakeholders benefit from audited financial information, including those who are not involved in hiring and compensating the auditor. There are free-riders who take advantage of auditing without paying for it. As a result, there is sub-optimal demand for the purchase of audits, and that can be used as an explanation for why auditing is imposed by legislation (Doty, 2014). Legislators in that case impose auditing requirements for the benefit of the community (Doty, 2014).

Yet another (and overlapping) explanation is that auditing is beneficial to a country's economy. Auditing can be seen as having positive externalities. Better private sector auditing is believed to be associated with better economic performance. The World Bank makes improving the auditing standards within a country a priority when making recommendations, e.g., in Argentina (The World Bank, 2007). A vice-president of the World Bank has described auditing as "an agent of transparency in development of an economy" (Muis, 1999). Similarly, studies of economic development include better auditing and accounting among measures of the investor protection environment, and have shown that they are associated with better economic performance. Rajan and Zingales (2001, 480) show that countries with better accounting have greater investment and more economic growth, and write: "a country intent on economic development should fix its financial plumbing." Kimbro (2002, 325) examines evidence that good accounting and auditing in general are good for a country's economy, using a model that links economic, cultural and information/monitoring variables to corruption in 61 countries. Inter alia, financial accounting systems are associated with low corruption. Evidence about the value of an auditing profession is provided by the differing impact of an economic crisis: for example, the Asian economic crisis of the 1990s. Those countries that had better-established auditing professions were able to shake off the effects of the Asian economic crisis more quickly (according to Muis, 1999). These two explanations show that mandatory auditing is imposed because it is in the public interest.

Since the Sarbanes-Oxley Act was passed in the US, most Western countries have introduced similar requirements for independent audit standard setting bodies and inspection of audits. Baker et al. (2014) describe these changes in selected countries, applying the institutional theory model described earlier and interpreting it as showing that the changes in France were consistent with mimetic isomorphism, while those in Canada were consistent with normative isomorphism.

An alternative set of views about regulation considers the incentives of those who can impose regulated auditing, either elected representatives or bureaucrats appointed by them, or independent standard setters. These explanations are more in line with public choice economics, and take into account the self-interest of the regulators themselves. If an audit failure is controversial, especially if it causes harm to voters, there will be an incentive for these powerful groups to impose further regulation. Ball (2009, 289) argues that such groups have an incentive to regulate in order to avoid perceived responsibility for investor losses, and that any legislative action is a political attempt to escape blame. Similar arguments are made by Watts and Zimmerman (1986). Ball (2009) depicts the Sarbanes-Oxley Act as a "rushed" attempt by Congress and President Bush to avoid being held responsible for the audit failures of the early twenty-first century.[6] In auditing, there appears to be a continuing cycle of increases in regulation in response to any problems that are seen as relating to auditing, and auditing has become much more highly regulated over the last 100 years. This trend lends credibility to the public choice explanation.

Another area of research shows evidence that auditors lobby in their own self-interest (Ramanna, 2015, 72). Auditor lobbying is consistent with managing of auditor liability and regulation cost (and not with the preferences of the auditors' clients) (Allen, Ramanna, and Roychowdhury, 2018). The evidence is not very strong, however, and this as an area where there are opportunities for more research.

D Situations in which auditing is valuable

Most published research about auditing is concerned with companies, especially listed companies in Western countries (just as most of the preceding discussion is). However, auditing is important in many other settings and it is useful to consider them in understanding why it is valued. Other audits include audits in less-developed countries; audits of smaller, unlisted companies; audits of voluntary organizations, such as clubs or charities; auditing in the public sector, including local government, schools, public hospitals, and other governmental entities, as well as the central government itself; and audits of other types of information, such as reports on internal control, corporate social responsibility disclosures, and privacy.

Audits in less-developed countries are arguably a more important area for research, compared to audits in larger and more established markets. There are greater risks of corruption, and companies have fewer resources for governance and auditing (Millichamp and Taylor, 2018, 491). As a result, there are more opportunities for auditing researchers to make a contribution that might be valuable to financial report users or auditees. Nevertheless, research in less-developed countries is not widespread (Iskander and Chamlou, 2000; Hay, 2017).

Audits of smaller, unlisted companies and audits of voluntary organizations, such as clubs or charities, are also an area that is not extensively researched. These areas are of interest, too, because there appears to be more risk of auditing not working as it should, and because developments in technology are changing the costs of auditing; it may be that the cost-benefit ratio will shift in favor of more extensive auditing for small entities.

Auditing in the public sector, including local government, schools, public hospitals, and other governmental entities, as well as the central government itself, is an area in which there is extensive auditing, but rather limited research. According to Hay and Cordery (2018, 1), public sector auditing has not been as widely examined as it should. Some time ago, Banker, Cooper, and Potter (1992, 508) wrote that "researchers in accounting have not been responsive to the problems and opportunities associated with developments in government accounting," and this comment is still relevant. Nevertheless, the literature includes many valuable studies (e.g., Baber, 1983; Blume and Voigt, 2011; Brusca, Caperchione, Cohen, and Manes, 2015). In this field, the existing research can be divided into two streams: "alternative" or "contextual" research and mainstream research (Broadbent and Guthrie, 2008, 131). The alternative stream is quite extensive. It tends to use qualitative research approaches, eclectic approaches to theory or no theory at all, and some examination of institutional theory and stakeholder theory (Jacobs, 2012; Modell, 2013). Uniting the two streams of research has the potential to enhance understanding of auditing (Goddard, 2010).

Cordery and Hay (2018a) examine the relevance of the six explanations for the value of auditing discussed above (agency, signaling, insurance, management control, governance, and confirmation) to the public sector.

They comment on how agency relationships are particularly relevant in the public sector setting, and illustrate the discussion with this quotation:

"Democratic politics are easily viewed in principal-agent terms. Citizens are principals, politicians are their agents. Politicians are principals, bureaucrats are their agents. The whole of politics is therefore structured by a chain of principal-agent relationships, from citizen to politician to bureaucratic subordinate and on down the hierarchy to the lowest-level bureaucrats who actually deliver services to citizens."

(Moe, 1984, 765)

The authors conclude that there is evidence for the relevance of each of the explanations to government accounting, except for the confirmation hypothesis, which has not yet been examined (Hay and Cordery, 2018). Overall, agency and management control explanations have generally been drawn on, with some contention over which is most relevant. Public sector auditors, in some cases, have access to considerably more information about the views of stakeholders than that available to private sector auditors (Cordery and Hay, 2018a). Public value, and reporting on it, including audited reports, is increasingly important (Cordery and Hay, 2018b).

Beyond these settings, audits are potentially valuable in many other areas, like reports on internal control, corporate social responsibility (CSR) disclosures (Simnett, 2014), and privacy (Toy and Hay, 2015). Reporting by auditors on internal control in the United States was initially contentious, but is now becoming more accepted, and more countries are requiring it (Bedard and Graham, 2014, 312). Assurance of CSR reports is normally not a requirement, but there is a growing demand for assurance of these types of report (Simnett, 2014, 326). Integrated reporting is a growing area, and assurance over integrated reports is also being investigated (Simnett, 2014). Privacy auditing is also a growing area (Toy and Hay, 2015). These areas also have potential for further research and are further discussed later.

E Historical development of auditing

Historical evidence about auditing is consistent with the explanations set out above. As long ago as 1494, Pacioli, in his treatise on double-entry bookkeeping, recommended the appraisal of accounts by an independent person (Willekens, 2007, 4). Watts and Zimmerman (1986, 312) describe how voluntary auditing existed for 600 years in circumstances where there was a need for stewardship, as "part of the efficient technology for organizing firms." The auditors used by corporations changed, with the coming of the industrial revolution, from amateur shareholder representatives to professional firms. While it is sometimes perceived that audits of company financial statements came into existence because they were required by government regulation, for example in the UK in 1862 or the US in 1933, the historical evidence does not support this view (Watts and Zimmerman, 1983, 614). Watts and Zimmerman (1983) argue that the rise of professional auditors occurred due to changes in the market for audit services, specifically the increase in number, size, and complexity of companies (Watts and Zimmerman, 1983, 630). The creation of professional societies of accountants also contributed because it provided a means to certify the quality and independence of auditors (Watts and Zimmerman, 1983, 631).

Maltby (2009) indicates how the explanation by Watts and Zimmerman (1983) that auditing was desirable, as it reduced the risks inherent in agency relationships, is also helpful in explaining why auditors are still valued, even when auditing failures are evident. While auditing is regulated in most large-organization settings, it shows "extraordinary resilience" considering the failures associated with it (Maltby, 2009, 230). Auditors have also been described as "invulnerable to their own failure" (Power, 1994). This speaks to the overall benefit of auditing, even when delivered at a level that is less than perfect. This can be partially explained by the difficulty in observing the outcome of an audit and recognition that the entire model of auditing is built on an assumption of residual risk, i.e., no matter how good the audit, there is always some remaining risk that material misstatements can exist in a set of financial statements that have been examined by an auditor. This potential is specifically reflected in the "audit risk model" (as described in International Auditing and Assurance Standards Board, 2009; Public Company Accounting Oversight Board, 2010) that guides much of what an auditor does. The fact that auditors cannot reduce residual risk to zero is partially the cause of the so-called expectations gap between what an auditor can realistically accomplish and what the general public expects, especially when using hindsight after an audit failure has been revealed by circumstances. There is also an argument that the adoption of voluntary auditing took place partly as a means for companies to avoid other kinds of regulation, specifically to avoid having to disclose financial reports (Maltby, 2009, 230). Maltby suggests that later adoption of voluntary auditing mechanisms may also have been intended to pre-empt regulation being imposed.

Auditing in the public sector has also developed over a very long period. It developed in the United Kingdom from a fairly rudimentary process after the Magna Carta (1215), to a stronger basis after the Glorious Revolution (1689), and became more sophisticated in the mid-nineteenth century (Funnell, 1994; Cordery and Hay, 2018b). In its earlier stages, auditing of public sector expenditure was conducted on behalf of the executive, and was consistent with the management control function explanation of auditing.

As Parliament became relatively more powerful, the numerous agency relationships in government management became important, and auditing became a more independent function similar to the audit of listed companies and consistent with agency explanations. The picture of the value of auditing is a complex one. There are the seven explanations discussed earlier, and these are supported by varying levels of evidence. There are also the other complicating factors that influence auditing, together with the support provided by regulation that sometimes requires auditing, and the very wide range of settings in which auditing can take place.

Notes

1 For example, managers sometimes do not realize how an audit can be of benefit to them.
2 Some more specific definitions concentrate on investors, e.g., "a set of mechanisms through which outside investors protect themselves against expropriation" (Cooper et al., 1996), while others recognize a wider range of stakeholders including the community as a whole (Elliott, 1994).
3 Although there may be other explanations for the higher audit fees, e.g., more public information released that is financial, even if not directly related to the financial statements, may also suggest greater risk and greater audit effort.
4 A similar argument had been raised earlier by Sorter (1979, 4) who argued that "you cannot expect that financial statements provided fresh news at point of impact . . . They provide a mechanism which allows users to interpret new information as it comes along. By identifying certain crucial relationships, it allows users to interpret new sales data when it comes along in terms of what a change in sales means to Chrysler vs. General Motors. Statements allow users to determine the significance of a wage settlement. In addition, financial statements can be used to validate alternate information sources and users' predictions."
5 However, there are also "public choice" arguments in opposition to this view of regulation, which I discuss later in this section.
6 Whether the Sarbanes-Oxley Act as an innovation in regulation was ultimately helpful is itself an issue about which researchers disagree (Hart, 2009; Merino et al., 2010).

References

Abbott, L. J., S. Parker, G. F. Peters, and K. Raghunandan. 2003. The Association Between Audit Committee Characteristics and Audit Fees. *Auditing: A Journal of Practice & Theory* 22 (2): 17–32.

Abdel-khalik, A. R. 1993. Why Do Private Companies Demand Auditing? A Case for Organizational Loss of Control. *Journal of Accounting, Auditing & Finance* 8 (1): 31–52.

Adnan, S., C. van Staden, and D. C. Hay. 2010. Do Culture and Governance Structure Influence CSR Reporting Quality: Evidence From China, India, Malaysia and the United Kingdom. In *Proceedings of the 6th Asia Pacific Interdisciplinary Research in Accounting Conference*, 1–27. Sydney, NSW.

Allen, A. M., K. Ramanna, and S. Roychowdhury. 2018. Auditor Lobbying on Accounting Standards. *Journal of Law, Finance & Accounting*. Forthcoming.

Ashbaugh-Skaife, H., D. W. Collins, W. R. Kinney Jr, and R. LaFond. 2009. The Effect of Internal Control Deficiencies on Firm Risk and Cost of Equity Capital. *Journal of Accounting Research* 47 (1): 1–43.

Audousset-Coulier, S., A. Jeny, and L. Jiang. 2016. The Validity of Auditor Industry Specialization Measures. *Auditing: A Journal of Practice &Theory* 35 (1): 139–161.

Baber, W. R. 1983. Toward Understanding the Role of Auditing in the Public Sector. *Journal of Accounting and Economics* 5 (C): 213–227.

Baber, W. R., K. R. Kumar, and T. Verghese. 1995. Client Security Price Reactions to the Laventhol and Horwath Bankruptcy. *Journal of Accounting Research* 33 (2): 385.

Baker, C. R., J. Bédard, and C. Prat dit Hauret. 2014. The Regulation of Statutory Auditing: An Institutional Theory Approach. *Managerial Auditing Journal* 29 (5): 371–394.

Ball, R. 2009. Market and Political/Regulatory Perspectives on the Recent Accounting Scandals. *Journal of Accounting Research* 47 (2): 277–323.

Ball, R., and P. Brown. 1968. An Empirical Evaluation of Accounting Income Numbers. *Journal of Accounting Research* 6 (2): 159–178.

Ball, R., S. Jayaraman, and L. Shivakumar. 2012. Audited Financial Reporting and Voluntary Disclosure as Complements: A Test of the Confirmation Hypothesis. *Journal of Accounting and Economics* 53 (1–2): 136–166.

Banker, R. D., W. W. Cooper, and G. Potter. 1992. A Perspective on Research in Governmental Accounting. *The Accounting Review* 67 (3): 496–510.

Beatty, R. P. 1989. Auditor Reputation and the Pricing of Initial Public Offerings. *Accounting Review* 64 (4): 693.

Bédard, J. C., and T. Compernolle. 2014. The External Auditor and The Audit Committee. In *The Routledge Companion to Auditing*, edited by D. C. Hay, W. R. Knechel, and M. Willekens, 253–263. Abingdon, UK: Routledge.

Bedard, J. C., and L. Graham. 2014. Reporting on Internal Control. In *The Routledge Companion to Auditing*, edited by D. C. Hay, W. R. Knechel, and M. Willekens, 311–322. Abingdon, UK: Routldege.

Blackwell, D. W., T. R. Noland, and D. B. Winters. 1998. The Value of Auditor Assurance: Evidence From Loan Pricing. *Journal of Accounting Research* 36 (1): 57.

Blume, L., and S. Voigt. 2011. Does Organizational Design of Supreme Audit Institutions Matter? A Cross-Country Assessment. *European Journal of Political Economy* 27 (2): 215–229.

Broadbent, J., and J. E. Guthrie. 2008. Public Sector to Public Services: 20 Years of "Contextual" Accounting Research. *Accounting Auditing & Accountability Journal* 21 (2): 129–169.

Brown, D. L., S. Z. Shu, B. S. Soo, and G. M. Trompeter. 2013. The Insurance Hypothesis: An Examination of KPMG's Audit Clients Around the Investigation and Settlement of the Tax Shelter Case. *Auditing: A Journal of Practice & Theory* 32 (4): 1–24.

Brusca, I., E. Caperchione, S. Cohen, and R. Manes. 2015. *Public Sector Accounting and Auditing in Europe: The Challenge of Harmonization*. Basingstoke, UK: Palgrave Macmillan.

Carcello, J. V., D. R. Hermanson, T. L. Neal, and R. A. Riley Jr. 2002. Board Characteristics and Audit Fees. *Contemporary Accounting Research* 19 (3): 365–384.

Chow, C. W. 1982. The Demand for External Auditing: Size, Debt and Ownership Influences. *The Accounting Review* 57 (2): 272–291.

Chow, C. W., L. Kramer, and A. W. Wanda. 1988. The Environment of Auditing. In *Research Opportunities in Auditing: The Second Decade*, edited by A. R. Abdelkhalik, and I. Solomon, 155–184. Sarasota, FL: American Accounting Association: Auditing Section.

Cohen, J. R., G. Krishnamoorthy, and A. M. Wright. 2004. The Corporate Governance Mosaic and Financial Reporting. *Journal of Accounting Literature* 23: 87–152.

Cooper, D. J., B. Hinings, R. Greenwood, J. L. Brown, D. J. Cooper, B. Hinings, R. Greenwood, and J. L. Brown. 1996. Sedimentation and Transformation in Organizational Change: The Case of Canadian Law Firms. *Organization Studies* 17 (4): 623–647.

Cordery, C. J., and D. C. Hay. 2018a. Evidence About the Value of Public Sector Audit to Stakeholders. *SSRN*. https://ssrn.com/abstract=2895806

———. 2018b. Supreme Audit Institutions and Public Value: Demonstrating Relevance. *Financial Accountability & Management*. Accepted.

Craswell, A. T., J. R. Francis, and S. L. Taylor. 1995. Auditor Brand Name Reputations and Industry Specializations. *Journal of Accounting and Economics* 20 (3): 297–322.

Dedman, E., and A. Kausar. 2012. The Impact of Voluntary Audit on Credit Ratings: Evidence From Private UK Firms. *Accounting and Business Research* 42 (4): 397–418.

Deegan, C. 2014. *Financial Accounting Theory*. 4th ed. North Ryde, NSW: McGraw-Hill Education (Australia).

DiMaggio, P., and W. Powell. 1983. The Iron Cage Revisited: Institutional Isomorphism and Collective Rationality in Organizational Fields. *American Sociological Review* 48 (2): 147–160.

Doty, J. R. 2014. The Role of Audit in Economic Growth. In *US Chamber of Commerce the Future of Financial Reporting*, 1–10. Washington, DC: PCAOB.

Eilifsen, A., and M. Willekens. 2007. In the name of trust: Some thoughts about trust, audit quality and audit regulation in Europe. In *Auditing, Trust and Governance: Developing Regulation in Europe*, edited by R. Quick, S. Turley, and M. Willekens, 1–18. London: Routledge.

Elliott, R. K. 1994. The Future of Audits. *Journal of Accountancy* 178 (3): 74–82.

Evans, J. H., and J. M. Patton. 1987, May. Signaling and Monitoring in Public-Sector Accounting. *Journal of Accounting Research* 25: 130–158.

Francis, J. R., K. Reichelt, and D. Wang. 2005. The Pricing of National and City-Specific Reputations for Industry Expertise in the U.S. Audit Market. *Accounting Review* 80 (1): 113–126.

Funnell, W. 1994. Independence and the State Auditor in Britain: A Constitutional Keystone or a Case of Reified Imagery? *Abacus* 30 (2): 175–195.

Goddard, A. 2010. Contemporary Public Sector Accounting Research: An International Comparison of Journal Papers. *The British Accounting Review* 42 (2): 75–87.

Gore, A. K. 2004. The Effects of GAAP Regulation and Bond Market Interaction on Local Government Disclosure. *Journal of Accounting and Public Policy* 23 (1): 23–52.

Gray, R., R. Kouhy, and S. Lavers. 1995. Corporate Social and Environmental Reporting. *Accounting, Auditing & Accountability Journal* 8 (2): 47–77.

Hart, O. 2009. Regulation and Sarbanes-Oxley. *Journal of Accounting Research* 47 (2): 437–445.

Hay, D. C. 2003. Knowledge Transfer Costs and Dependence as Determinants of Financial Reporting. *Accounting and Finance* 43 (3): 311–330.

———. 2017. Opportunities for Auditing Research: Back to Our Interdisciplinary Roots. Ed. C. de Villiers and C. de Villiers. *Meditari Accountancy Research* 25 (3): 336–350.

Hay, D. C., and C. J. Cordery. 2018. The Value of Public Sector Audit: Literature and History. *Journal of Accounting Literature* 40: 1–15.

Hay, D. C., and D. Davis. 2004. The Voluntary Choice of an Auditor of Any Level of Quality. *Auditing: A Journal of Practice & Theory* 23 (2): 37–53.

Heald, D. 2018. Transparency-Generated Trust: The Problematic Theorization of Public Audit. *Financial Accountability & Management*: 1–19.

International Auditing and Assurance Standards Board. 2009. International Standard on Auditing 200: Overall Objectives of the Independent Auditor and the Conduct of an Audit in Accordance With International Standards on Auditing. In *Handbook of International Quality Control, Auditing Review, Other Assurance, and Related Services Pronouncements*. New York, NY: IFAC.

Iskander, M. R., and N. Chamlou. 2000. *Corporate Governance: A Framework for Implementation*. Washington, DC: The World Bank.

Jacobs, K. 2012. Making Sense of Social Practice: Theoretical Pluralism in Public Sector Accounting Research. *Financial Accountability & Management* 28 (1): 1–25.

Jensen, M. C., and W. H. Meckling. 1976. Theory of the Firm: Managerial Behavior, Agency Costs and Ownership Structure. *Journal of Financial Economics* 3 (4): 305–360.

Khurana, I. K., and K. K. Raman. 2004. Litigation Risk and the Financial Reporting Credibility of Big 4 Versus Non-Big 4 Audits: Evidence From Anglo-American Countries. *The Accounting Review* 79 (2): 473–495.

Kimbro, M. B. 2002. A cross-country empirical investigation of corruption and its relationship to economic, cultural, and monitoring institutions: An examination of the role of accounting and financial statements quality. *Journal of Accounting, Auditing and Finance* 17 (4): 325–343.

Knechel, W. R., and M. Willekens. 2006. The Role of Risk Management and Governance in Determining Audit Demand. *Journal of Business Finance and Accounting* 33 (9–10): 1344–1367.

Langli, J. C., and M. Willekens. 2017. Tax Avoidance , Horizontal Agency Conflicts and High-Quality Auditing in Private Firms. In *Scandinavian Accounting Research Conference*. Oslo.

Lawrence, A., M. Minutti-Meza, and P. Zhang. 2011. Can Big 4 Versus Non-Big 4 Differences in Audit-Quality Proxies be Attributed to Client Characteristics? *Accounting Review* 86 (1): 259–286.

Lennox, C. S., and J. A. Pittman. 2011. Voluntary Audits Versus Mandatory Audits. *Accounting Review* 86 (5): 1655–1678.

Maltby, J. 2008. There Is No Such Thing as Audit Society: A Reading of Power, M. (1994a) "The Audit Society". *Ephemera* 8 (4): 388–398.

———. 2009. Auditing. In *The Routledge Companion to Accounting History*, edited by J. R. Edwards, and S. P. Walker, 224–244. Abingdon, UK: Routledge.

Mansi, S. A., W. F. Maxwell, and D. P. Miller. 2004. Does Auditor Quality and Tenure Matter to Investors? Evidence From the Bond Market. *Journal of Accounting Research* 42 (4): 755–793.

Menon, K., and D. D. Williams. 1994. The Insurance Hypothesis and Market Prices. *Accounting Review* 69 (2): 327–342.

Merino, B. D., A. G. Mayper, and T. D. Tolleson. 2010. Neoliberalism, Deregulation and Sarbanes-Oxley: The Legitimation of a Failed Corporate Governance Model. *Accounting, Auditing and Accountability Journal* 23 (6): 774–792.

Millichamp, A., and J. Taylor. 2018. *Auditing.* 11th ed. Andover, UK: Cengage.

Modell, S. 2013. Making Sense of Social Practice: Theoretical Pluralism in Public Sector Accounting Research: A Comment. *Financial Accountability & Management* 29 (1): 99–110.

Moe, T. M. 1984. The New Economics of Organization. *American Journal of Political Science* 28 (4): 739–777.

Muis, J. 1999. Accounting and Transparency. In *Asia-Pacific Conference on International Accounting Issues*. Melbourne: California State University, Fresno.

Ortas, E., I. Álvarez, J. Jaussaud, and A. Garayar. 2015. The Impact of Institutional and Social Context on Corporate Environmental, Social and Governance Performance of Companies Committed to Voluntary Corporate Social Responsibility Initiatives. *Journal of Cleaner Production* 108: 673–684.

Pacini, C., W. Hillison, R. Alagiah, and S. Gunz. 2002. Commonwealth Convergence Toward a Narrower Scope of Auditor Liability to Third Parties for Negligent Misstatements. *Abacus* 38 (3): 425–464.

Palmrose, Z.-V. 1988. An Analysis of Auditor Litigation and Audit Service Quality. *The Accounting Review* 63 (1): 55–73.

Pincus, K., M. Rusbarsky, and J. Wong. 1989. Voluntary Formation of Corporate Audit Committees Among NASDAQ Firms. *Journal of Accounting and Public Policy* 8 (4): 239–265.

La Porta, R., F. Lopez-de-Silanes, A. Shleifer, and R. Vishny. 2000. Investor Protection and Corporate Governance. *Journal of Financial Economics* 58 (1–2): 3–27.

Power, M. K. 1994. *The Audit Explosion*. London, UK: Demos.

———. 2000. The Audit Society: Second Thoughts. *International Journal of Auditing* 4 (1): 111–119.

Public Company Accounting Oversight Board. 2010. Auditing Standards Related to the Auditor's Assessment of and Response to Risk. In *Public Company Accounting Oversight Board*, 291. Washington, DC: PCAOB.

Rajan, R. G., and L. Zingales. 2001. Financial Systems, Industrial Structure, and Growth. *Oxford Review of Economic Policy* 17 (4): 467–482.

Ramanna, K. 2015. The Shrinking Big N: Rule-Making Incentives of the Tightening Oligopoly in Auditing. In *Political Standards: Corporate Interest, Ideology, and*

Leadership in the Shaping of Accounting Rules for the Market Economy, edited by K. Ramanna, 68–85. Chicago, IL: University of Chicago Press.

Şabac, F., and J. Tian. 2015. On the Stewardship Value of Soft Managerial Reports. *Accounting Review* 90 (4): 1683–1706.

Salamon, G. L., and D. S. Dhaliwal. 1980. Company Size and Financial Disclosure Requirements With Evidence From the Segmental Reporting Issue. *Journal of Business Finance & Accounting* 7 (4): 555–568.

Shore, C., and S. Wright. 2015. Governing by Numbers: Audit Culture, Rankings and the New World Order. *Social Anthropology* 23 (1): 22–28.

Simnett, R. 2014. Assurance of Environment, Social and Sustainability Information. In *The Routledge Companion to Auditing*, edited by D. C. Hay, W. R. Knechel, and M. Willekens, 325–337. Abingdon, UK: Routledge.

Simunic, D. A. 1980. The Pricing of Audit Services: Theory and Evidence. *Journal of Accounting Research* 18 (1): 161.

———. 2014. The Market for Audit Services. In *The Routledge Companion to Auditing*, edited by D. C. Hay, W. R. Knechel, and M. Willekens, 33–42. Abingdon, UK: Routledge.

Sorter, G. H. 1979, 27 March. *Beyond Emptiness and Blindness: Is There a Hope for Accounting Research?* Speech, 27 March 1979, London School of Economics. http://wiki.phalkefactory.net/images/7/78/BEYOND_EMPTINESS_AND_BLINDNESS-_hope_for_accounting_research.pdf.

Srinidhi, B. N., S. He, and M. Firth. 2014. The Effect of Governance on Specialist Auditor Choice and Audit Fees in U.S. Family Firms. *Accounting Review* 89 (6): 2297–2329.

Teoh, S. H., and T. J. Wong. 1993. Perceived Auditor Quality and the Earnings Response Coefficient. *The Accounting Review* 68 (2): 346–366.

Titman, S., and B. Trueman. 1986. Information Quality and the Valuation of New Issues. *Journal of Accounting and Economics* 8: 159–172.

Toy, A., and D. C. Hay. 2015. Privacy Auditing Standards. *Auditing: A Journal of Practice & Theory* 34 (3): 181–199.

Wallace, W. A. 1980. *The Economic Role of the Audit in Free and Regulated Markets*. New York NY.: Touche Ross Foundation.

Wallace, W. A. 1987. The Economic Role of the Audit in Free and Regulated Markets. *Advances in Accounting* 1: 7–34.

Watts, R. L., and J. L. Zimmerman. 1983. Agency Problems, Auditing, and the Theory of the Firm: Some Evidence. *The Journal of Law and Economics* 26 (3): 613–633.

———. 1986. *Positive Accounting Theory*. Engelwood Cliffs, NJ: Prentice-Hall.

Willekens, M. 2007. *To Audit or Not to Audit? On the Use of Auditing in a Continental European Setting*. Tilburg: Tilburg University.

Willekens, M., A. Steele, and D. Miltz. 1996. Audit standards and auditor liability: A theoretical model. *Accounting and Business Research* 26 (3): 249–264.

Willenborg, M. 1999. Empirical Analysis of the Economic Demand for Auditing in the Initial Public Offerings Market. *Journal of Accounting Research* 37 (1): 225–238.

The World Bank. 2007. *Report on the Observance of Standards and Codes (ROSC) - Accounting and Auditing. Report No. AAA35-AR Argentina*.

Zimmerman, J. L. 1977. The Municipal Accounting Maze: An Analysis of Political Incentives. *Journal of Accounting Research* 15: 107–144.

3 The future of auditing

Auditing is unusually complex, and some issues arise from that complexity that can probably never be resolved. Auditing is complex because of the challenges of organizing highly skilled professionals to undertake a task that carries great responsibility; of continuing to maintain high standards and develop new techniques in order to meet the changing needs of business; and of meeting the needs of diverse stakeholders. The way in which these issues are dealt with has changed in recent decades, and I suggest that the changes give insight into how auditing may develop in the future. Current developments that extend into the future will make a difference, too. In particular, auditing in the future might need to respond to:

- Global trends in demographics and economics
- Trends in accounting and auditing
- Information technology and automation
- Global, not national, auditing (and standard setting)
- Evidence-based standard setting and development
- Relevant audits for a wide variety of stakeholders
- Changes to the partnership model of audit firms

A Global trends

Predicting the future involves taking account of global trends that already seem to be well established and underway. A few of these trends are aging of the population, climate change, and change and growth in information technology.

There is increasing longevity in the developed world (Maestas and Zissimopoulos, 2010; Kontis et al., 2017). As a result, there is a rising trend of interest in saving for retirement, and in pensions. This trend seems likely to make financial statements, and therefore audits of financial statements, of increasing importance. Longer life-spans are associated with those people wanting to save (Modigliani and Brumberg, 1954), making investments, and needing assurance about the financial statements of the entities they are investing in.

There is also increased equality of income among nations – the middle-income countries of the world, which include India and China, have a much larger share of the world's GDP in 2011 than they did in 2005 (World Bank Group, 2015). China and India, especially, are developing larger and stronger economies. It is reasonable to expect increasing demand for auditing in these countries. The issues of multinational auditors of multinational corporations and the need for a multinational regulator will become even more apparent when there are numerous "great powers" instead of the present environment dominated by Europe and North America (and Australasia). In addition, there are still many less-developed countries, many with fast-growing populations. As countries develop economically, they are in many cases also globalizing and adopting institutions that exist in Western countries – auditing is likely to be one of these technologies. There is likely to be increased demand for auditing, but not necessarily in the same places as now.

On the other hand, the rising interest in saving and therefore reliable financial reporting is counteracted to some extent by other trends. For example, individuals and families are now much less likely to invest directly in shares and to conduct their own research, and more likely to invest in index funds (e.g., Ellis, 2017). As a result of that trend, there is a smaller audience for financial reports and audits, although that audience is nevertheless substantial and more sophisticated than most individual investors. Another contrary trend is contemporary changes to the news media. In the "new media environment," most news media organizations are operating with reduced staff and other resources. As a result, the media have less interest in investigative journalism (Walton, 2010). Other changes in the new media environment include more internationalization, new communications techniques, and trends for journalists to present a more personal viewpoint (Liebes and Kampf, 2009). These trends have reduced news coverage of routine matters, like audit reports and investigations, into business scandals.

Climate change is a widely accepted phenomenon. A related question is whether this will trigger more emphasis on environmental auditing. In addition, the world is in an age of education. On average, the populations of developed countries are more educated than ever before (Organization for Economic Cooperation and Development (OECD), 2013). Masters degrees are seen as a measure of the status of an occupation. This trend affects auditors in two ways: users of financial reports are likely to become more sophisticated, and the status of chartered accountants or CPAs may decline relative to other occupations, especially in those countries like the UK, Australia, or New Zealand where the highest university qualification that auditors are likely to have is a bachelor's degree (in contrast to other countries, where professional accountants generally do have higher degrees).

In a report prepared for KPMG on global mega-trends affecting governments, higher life expectancy and concern among aging citizens about pensions, economic interconnectedness, and the economic power shift towards emerging economies were among the trends identified (KPMG International, 2013). These three mega-trends will also affect the demand for auditing and the nature of it. Increased life expectancy and the rise of emerging economies are discussed in this section; economic interconnectedness is part of the next section, globalization. What else is changing in the world?

• Technology (discussed in section D, Information Technology and Automation)
• Surprising political developments. These include election results which were not expected, including Brexit or President Trump. In a different category, but nevertheless a change, is the rise of political leaders from a new generation, such as Macron in France, Trudeau in Canada, and Ardern in New Zealand. These developments show how difficult predicting the future is

To summarize, the future of auditing will take place in a changing world. Auditors are struggling to keep up in some areas, but there are many changes that have the potential to make auditing more important.

B Trends in accounting and auditing

There has been a longstanding trend for accounting information to be supplemented, or even supplanted, by other sources of information (Percy, 1999, 82; Accountancy Europe, 2017). FEE (the Fédération des Experts-comptables Européens, which later became Accountancy Europe) suggested deepening the role of audit professionals to add value in financial and non-financial information (Fédération des Experts-comptables Européens, 2014). FEE subsequently suggested that auditors need to enhance their engagement with stakeholders to demonstrate their ability to meet their needs with new forms of assurance; to harness the benefits of technology; and to adapt the education of future auditors to a changing environment (Fédération des Experts-comptables Européens, 2016, 3). A study by Forbes Insights for the Global Public Policy Committee (of the six largest global accounting firms) concluded that audits are valuable, and "nobody can imagine the world without the audit," but that auditing needs to evolve to provide more information to users (Forbes Insight, 2015, 13).

The expectation gap, between the expectations of the society about the performance of financial report auditors and what is perceived to be delivered, is a related issue (Porter, 2014, 43). The expectation gap is conventionally broken down into three components, representing gaps because auditors do not follow the standards required, because the standards are not consistent with reasonable expectations, and unreasonable beliefs by users who do not understand auditing. These are the deficient performance gap, deficient standards gap, and unrealistic expectations gap. It can be argued that the expectation gap will never be resolved – so long as people compare an auditor's ex ante opinion to ex post outcomes, there will always be an expectation gap. Hindsight bias ensures that auditors will always be held responsible for issues that they were unlikely to have been to detect in advance. The more important issue is likely to be whether auditors work to a "reasonable" (i.e., Pareto-efficient) level of residual risk (or assurance) and whether they achieve that target. The expectation gap is thus an issue needing continual attention. It also serves as a map of the future path of auditing regulation, allowing predictions to be made about forthcoming changes. For example, users have higher expectations that auditors will detect and report going concern problems. Auditing standards have shown a trend to increase auditors' responsibility about this issue, and this will probably continue.

Recent research shows that the audit expectation gap is not static, and tends to get worse when regulations are not continually changed (Porter, Hógartaigh, and Baskerville, 2012). The study by Porter et al. (2012) showed evidence that the extent of the disparity between user expectations and auditor performance had remained approximately the same in the UK, even though there had been extensive reforms to auditing. In New Zealand, where there had been minimal change, the overall expectation gap had increased. In both cases, the deficient standards gap had decreased to some extent, while the impact on the deficient standards gap and unrealistic expectations gap had been an overall decrease in the UK and increase in New Zealand (Porter et al., 2012, 215).

Assurance of other issues apart from financial report auditing is a very broad, and rapidly expanding, area. This area includes other assurance activities, such as quality auditing, as well as new areas that have grown out of the financial audit function. The wider area of quality auditing includes audits of quality control, which have their own professional experts, their own standards, and their own professional literature.

Quality control audits and similar activities are long-established. They have experienced rapid growth. These audits are often conducted under standards such as ISO 9000 (Karapetrovic and Willborn, 2002). There appear to have been few, if any, attempts by researchers in the area of financial report auditing to apply auditing research to these audits, or to learn from them. There are likely to be opportunities for new ideas and growth in these areas. However, there are shared areas of interest, such as corporate social responsibility (Alsaif, Savage, and Reed, 2018).

Other areas, such as reporting by auditors on a firm's internal control structure, or on environmental sustainability, have grown out of financial report auditing, either through regulation or from the development of voluntary practices.

Auditing of internal control is a practice that is required by law in some jurisdictions, including China (Wang, Xu, and Zeng, 2014) and Japan (Nakashima and Ziebart, 2015), as well as the US. It is likely to spread. Reporting on internal control when introduced in the United States was not particularly welcome to auditors or company managers, but now seems to be well accepted (Bedard and Graham, 2014). Should reporting on internal control continue to spread to other countries, especially in Europe and in New Zealand, Australia, and the United Kingdom? This additional assurance is expensive, but the alternative – that companies looking after money invested by the public are permitted to have internal control weaknesses – is also not appealing. It is reasonable to expect that this extension of financial report auditing will spread to other countries.

New forms of auditing are being demanded. Environmental auditing is an area that has developed from at one time being seen as a somewhat eccentric disclosure in unusual and particular cases, to becoming now a more mainstream activity. Environmental auditing is now discussed in textbooks as well as research papers (e.g., Gay and Simnett, 2015). Accountants might be asked to "save the world," environmentally (Wammes, 2016; Bakker, 2013). Integrated reporting <IR> is an innovation that appears to have caught on, but how to provide assurance over this information is still not clear (IIRC, 2014). Its proponents argue that it leads to integrated thinking, which becomes a force for financial stability and sustainability (IIRC, 2014, 4).

What other forms of additional auditing might be introduced? Privacy auditing is one form imposed on some organizations by a regulator, for example by the FTC in the US on Google and Facebook (Hill, 2011). In those two cases, the US Federal authorities required these entities to undergo privacy audits every two years. The agency did not suggest where privacy audits might be obtained from, but the media speculated that the major audit firms were the obvious choice (Hill, 2011). Google did indeed turn to PwC for their privacy audit (PwC, 2012). Privacy is a very contentious issue, and privacy auditing may grow as a response to the problems (Toy and Hay, 2015). Auditing has been described as "about to become the principal means by which democratic societies protect themselves from the tyranny of big data" (Malmgren, 2017, 26).

A privacy audit that is available in the public domain is one that PwC conducted for Google (Toy and Hay, 2015; PwC, 2012). The report provides assurance applying the IAASB's International Framework for Assurance Engagements and so has similarities to a financial audit report. It describes the assertions made by Google management about privacy, and then gives the auditor's opinion on the assertions. Other privacy audit reports that are in the public domain vary widely.

Combined assurance is another innovation in auditing in which the audit committee and the auditors report jointly. It was developed in South Africa and is becoming more widely known. Zhou, Simnett, and Hoang, (2018) report that the use of combined assurance reduces analysts' forecast errors and reduces bid-ask spreads.

Another major issue within auditing is how to achieve innovation while ensuring high standards. There are two issues: keeping to the formal standards that exist, and improving standards and practices for the future. Research and development – finding ways for auditors to continue to develop new techniques in order to meet the changing needs of business – has an inherent difficulty. The auditing profession's approach to the two parts of this problem (enforcement of standards and development of standards) usually includes increasing levels of regulatory inspection and compliance, and requiring auditing to be done to comply with generally accepted auditing standards. This is a conservative approach which has limitations. Auditors (especially in common-law jurisdictions) are expected to conduct their work to the standard of a reasonable auditor. It is common when an auditor is accused of negligence for another auditor to be asked to give evidence about the work that he or she might have done in the same situation. This approach dates back to a nineteenth-century case in the United Kingdom.[1] Asking auditors to conduct their work to a standard that is generally accepted has a conservative bias, and it is not a great way to develop new techniques. Auditors take a greater risk of liability by trying to develop new and better techniques for collecting evidence than they do by sticking to the tried and true methods. As a result, any extensions to auditor responsibility often come from regulations imposed by government or professional bodies, not from developments by auditors themselves. Auditors might also argue that their exposure to a high risk of liability also imposes a restriction on their ability to do anything new, providing another limitation to the ability of auditing to develop as it should in a complex and changing world.

It can be argued that regulating demand is inefficient because demand for auditing exists without regulation (as discussed in the "value of auditing" section of this book). Standards can the undermine the economic value of the audit, and lead to fee pressures, as argued by Knechel (2013). Nevertheless, given that audit quality is not observable, standards and regulations that put a floor on quality are critical. However, it is also the case that regulation has unintended consequences, including costs and inefficiencies (Knechel, 2016, 220). These include excessive focus on the compliance of an audit with the formal standards, rather than the assurance achieved; auditors concentrating on meeting the expectations of inspectors at the expense of substantive auditing issues; overly standardized audits; and reduced quality due to decreased use of professional judgment.

In response to issues like the global financial crisis, there were many proposals for improvements to auditing. Major proposals in 2013 included the IAASB consultation paper on audit quality (IAASB, 2013a) and the exposure draft on audit reports (IAASB, 2013b; IAASB, 2015). The IAASB audit quality document raises ten issues for exploration, and some of them deal with the problems of maintaining high quality in the unusual environment of auditing. Issues such as the culture of the audit firm are brought up: "appropriate values, ethics, and attitude." The completed document incorporates these factors (IAASB, 2014).

The IAASB's document on audit reporting, "Improving the Auditor's Report" (International Auditing and Assurance Standards Board, 2012), suggested dramatic changes to the information included in an audit report, including a commentary by the audit partner that gives some detail about the important issues in the audit (and the audit partner signing in his or her own name as well as the name of the firm). Some audit partners viewed these proposals with dread (e.g., Posner, 2017). They considered that the proposed changes would inhibit communication between management and auditor, expose the auditor to unduly high liability, or simply be too difficult, so that they might result in a fairly meaningless boilerplate report.

The initiative to introduce enhanced audit reports was based on research studies commissioned by the IAASB (e.g., Mock, Turner, Gray, and Coram, 2009). According to the IAASB, the proposals are supported by financial report users, particularly investors and analysts, and IAASB argues that similar changes will be useful to other users (IAASB, 2015). These changes are now substantially in place in most countries, and a form of the new enhanced audit reports will soon be issued in the United States as well (Public Company Accounting Oversight Board, 2017). Research studies on the enhanced audit report show some evidence from the UK and New Zealand that financial reporting quality improved (Li, Hay, and Lau, 2019; Reid, Carcello, Li, and Neal, 2018). There is some evidence that audit fees increased in New Zealand (Bradbury and Almulla, 2018; Li et al., 2019), but not in the UK (Reid et al., 2018). On the other hand, the new reports in the UK did not appear to provide incremental information to investors (Lennox, Schmidt, and Thompson, 2015; Gutierrez, Minutti-Meza, Tatum, and Vulcheva, 2018). The audit report is a unique issue, because it deals with the aspects of an audit that are in public view. The use of research to inform developments in audit standard setting is nevertheless encouraging to researchers.

C Information technology and automation

A survey and focus group study by a subsidiary of the AICPA (Canton and Institute for Global Futures, 2015) suggested that future technology innovations that will be an important influence include 3D manufacturing, digital money, smart machines, the internet of things, and digital distribution. The study, like a number of others referred to in this section, concluded that American CPAs did not fully recognize the role that technology will play in the future. The same study also pointed to the changing workforce, which is becoming more diverse, and the global marketplace as the middle classes in African and Asia become substantially more wealthy.

"Digital money," including crypto-currencies, is still in an experimental stage, and so are the blockchains or distributed ledgers that support these currencies but that can be used for other record-keeping activities. The use of blockchains can make transaction recording more secure and eliminate the need to reconcile differences between clients and the firms they do business with (Raj, 2017; Millichamp and Taylor, 2018, 489). Their long-term effects cannot yet be predicted (Choudhury, 2014), but there are some strongly negative comments about the impact of the blockchain on auditing (e.g., Arrowsmith, 2018).

A working session by CPA Canada suggested that changes taking place include: greater access to information by individuals, so that any individual has access to information that might attest to the viability of an investment, independent of the audit process; increasing complexity of accounting and financial reporting; and that new measures such as the management discussion and analysis, and environmental sustainability, are increasingly important and there is increasing demand for assurance over them (CPA Canada, 2013).

It is generally accepted among professional accounting institutes and major firms that technological changes are going to lead to dramatic change in auditing (ICAEW, 2018; Millichamp and Taylor, 2018, 489). Audits "need to adapt to the digital age" (Jeffrey and Gambier, 2016, 11).

The major international auditing firms are making some progress in adapting to the digital age. They have technology platforms to help them manage their audits and communicate progress; analytic techniques to identify issues; ways to handle big data and conduct audits that are more effective than ever before; and new auditing tools (Anderson, 2017). Examples of the auditing technology that firms are disclosing include for example PwC (2018). Tools used by auditors also include confirmations online via third parties using applications like confirmation.com (Hanes, Porco, and Thibodeau, 2014; Brown-Liburd and Vasarhelyi, 2015).

Accounting firms also sometimes point to the use of drones to inspect inventory quantities as an innovation (Harris, 2017; Rowland, 2018). Discussions of this technique appear in the news, and a recent Financial Times (UK) article suggested that auditors have already reached the stage where frontline audit staff do not need to "spend balance dates in draughty warehouses counting inventory" (Marriage, 2017; Murphy, 2017). It may be the case that articles like this are overstating the extent to which this technique is in use as yet.

Technology can solve some existing problems for auditors, particularly when there are very large volumes of transactions. New software techniques are widely predicted to allow auditors to use technology to examine all of the data, not merely a small sample (Susskind and Susskind, 2015, 91; Millichamp and Taylor, 2018, 489). Other innovations are likely to include data analytics and machine learning (Shimamoto, 2018). Continuous auditing is another innovation that has been on the horizon for some time (Holderness, 2014). Thompson (2017) warns that accountants, especially in small and medium practices, will be affected by digital technology.

There are many innovations that will affect accounting and auditing, but they do not seem to be coming fast. Susskind and Susskind (2015) suggests that change to auditing is taking place at a slower pace compared to similar disciplines (e.g., tax) because of the conservatism of regulators, and because the dominance of the Big 4 firms gives them no obvious incentive to change the status quo (Susskind and Susskind, 2015, 89). There are other sources, including those from accounting bodies, which concur that auditing has not kept pace with technological developments (Byrnes et al., 2012).

There is further evidence that users and other participants in auditing think that auditors are slow to take up new technologies. A survey reported that large numbers believe that "auditors should use advanced technology more extensively: 70% of users, 76% of audit committees, 84% of preparers (Deloitte, 2016). Another study in which KPMG participated found similar results. "Nearly 80% of respondents say auditors should use bigger samples and more sophisticated technologies for data gathering and analysis" (Forbes, 2017, 3).

There are also grounds for concern that professional standards are restricting technological change. The International Federation of Accountants (IFAC) concluded that although ISAs do not prohibit the use of modern data analytics techniques in auditing, they do not permit or encourage them either (IAASB Data Analytics Working Group, 2016). The regulations do not directly deter auditors from innovation – the standards neither "prohibit, nor stimulate the use of data analytics" for example (IAASB Data Analytics

Working Group, 2016, 8). However, firms developing new techniques are taking a risk that inspectors of their work will not understand the innovative approach and regard it as a deficiency.

The ICAEW "Future of Audit" project identifies the need for audit firms, professional bodies, and regulators to understand technological developments that will transform auditing in areas including audit testing of complete populations instead of samples, greater use of analytics, and continuous auditing (ICAEW, 2017). They also refer to the blockchain.

A commonly held view by auditors seems to be something like the following, from a speech by a member of the Public Company Accounting Oversight Board (PCAOB) in the US. About technology, he said: "As powerful as these tools are, or are expected to become, they nonetheless are not substitutes for the auditor's knowledge, judgment and exercise of professional skepticism" (Harris, 2017). This view appears to be held widely by accounting firms and accountants. That is a comforting thought, but it is not necessarily realistic. Instead, according to Susskind and Susskind (2015, 276), "high performing machines will outperform the best human experts." These authors point out that for automation to outperform humans, the technology does not need to act in the same way as a person does. There may be other ways of getting the task done, like just running a calculation on all of the possible outcomes. There are already examples in medicine. Computers that beat experts at sophisticated games like chess illustrate how this can be done.

There is a lot of potential for change in auditing technology. Auditors are moving to take advantage of it, but there are barriers, and it is reasonable to query whether they will they be able to adapt to the digital age. To summarize, accountants and professional bodies are aware of impending changes in this area, but not necessarily aware of what to do.

D Global or national auditing

Globalization of auditing is a longstanding trend, but it is not without complications, and these appear to be increasing. Auditing has been an international activity for a long time, arguably since British auditors were engaged to report to British investors on the audits of American companies in the nineteenth century (Maltby, 2009, 237). Since then, the influence of the global firm networks has been important, and in recent years, international standards and cooperation between the International Auditing and Assurance Standards Board and the US Public Company Accounting Oversight Board have made most areas of auditing fairly similar around the world. The extent to which auditing globally can reach convergence appears to be reaching its limits, however. Important issues are variations in how auditing practices are applied in different cultural settings, and the collision of different regulatory bodies, especially regarding inspection of auditing work. Francis (2011) points out that although there are global accounting firms, they are each made up of country-specific partnerships. Each country has its own systems of education, licensing, and regulation, and more subtle differences in areas such as the extent to which auditors will be skeptical. The education of auditors, cultural differences, and varying perceptions of the function of auditing across countries, as well as the legal framework and the political, economic, and business framework, are likely to make auditing very different according to what country it is practiced in (Francis, 2011, 321). As a result, it is not likely that the quality of auditing is the same everywhere – or that research findings are generalizable, either (Francis, 2011). Part of the role of the International Auditing Standards (ISAs) is to ensure standardization, but their application nevertheless depends on local interpretations (Humphrey, Loft, and Samsonova-Taddei, 2014).

Studies that examine auditing across countries have shown that when different countries are compared, audit fees reflect variations in the legal regime and the exposure of auditors to litigation risk (Choi, Kim, Liu, and Simunic, 2008; Jaggi and Low, 2011; Srinidhi, Hossain, and Lim, 2012). Nikkinen and Sahlström (2004) demonstrate that the agency theory can explain international variations in audit pricing. Other influences include rules on disclosure and regulation (Taylor and Simon, 1999), culture and trust in society (Knechel, Mintchik, Pevzner, and Velury, 2018), and the overall level of development of a country (Chung and Narasimhan, 2002). Eierle, Hartlieb, Hay, Niemi, and Ojala (2018) report that litigation risk in a jurisdiction, the general trust in major companies within a society, and the market share of Big 4 audit firms influence differing levels of auditing fees among countries. Stronger investment protection increases the earnings quality of reports audited by Big 4 audit firms (Francis and Wang, 2008), whereas there is evidence that market concentration within the group of Big 4 works in the opposite direction and is associated with reduced quality (Francis, Michas, and Seavey, 2013).

Studies of the audit profession in emerging market countries show that audit quality is higher in countries with a more developed auditing profession (Michas, 2011, 1731). There are sizable differences across different environments worldwide. Development of the auditing profession is measured by reports compiled by the World Bank (the Reports on Standards and Codes, or ROSC) and the International Federation of Accountants (IFAC) (Michas, 2011, 1736). In turn, the auditing environment influences development aid loans by the World Bank, although whether the country is geo-politically aligned with the United States also influences these results (Lamoreaux, Michas, and Schultz, 2015, 703).

The most striking change to auditor regulation in the twenty-first century has been the change from self-regulation to independent regulation in most jurisdictions (Carson, 2014, 24; Offermans and Vanstraelen, 2014, 185). Auditing regulation and oversight has undoubtedly improved. Scandals still occur, so that oversight and inspection are still important issues. In the existing world of national jurisdictions, there are quality issues and issues of the structure of regulation that make overview and inspection more difficult. Recent issues regarding US-listed companies in China, where there are restrictions on the ability of the PCAOB to access auditors' working papers (and a continuing impasse), provide an illustration of the problems that can occur (Carson, 2014; Reuters Staff, 2017; Rapoport and Dummett, 2012). There are several other countries where the PCAOB has been prevented from conducting inspections (e.g., Austria, Belgium, Poland, and Portugal) (Van Linden and Mazza, 2018). In these circumstances, multinational regulation, including oversight and inspection, may never be achieved. Differences in audit quality are likely to persist.

There is some international cooperation among the bodies that oversee auditors, particularly through the International Federation of Independent Audit Regulators (IFIAR). IFIAR's focus is on cooperation among national regulators (International Forum of Independent Audit Regulators, 2018) and it does not have a role as a supranational regulator.

Other approaches to auditing than the current system of private, regulated audit firms have been considered. Francis (2011) refers to other forms of certification that exist in the world, such as ISO standards, and to a proposal discussed by the US Congress in 2001 for audits to be carried out by a state-run Federal Bureau of Audits. Future developments might include radical changes like these.

E Evidence-based auditing standards

Standard setters are increasingly aware of research on auditing issues that could be relevant to their work. Recent changes such as the enhanced audit report have been influenced by research. The complexity of research results and the variety of inconsistent results in the published literature makes the application of research to auditing difficult, however. The "ambiguity problem," which is widespread in social science, occurs where potential users of research such as standard setters find it difficult to apply research that has a mixture of significant and insignificant results, some positive and some negative. Standard setters are more likely to demand a synthesis. Systematic research reviews, including meta-analyses, are used in many disciplines to help deal with the ambiguity problem. However, these systematic approaches are surprisingly infrequent in auditing research. Some of the top journals, for example the *Journal of Accounting and Economics*, appear to prefer narrative literature reviews. Narrative reviews are subject to major limitations, because they are influenced by the preconceptions and preferences of their authors.

In auditing, the PCAOB and the auditing research community developed papers that synthesize existing research to provide useful information for future regulatory action (Cohen and Knechel, 2013). Subsequently, the PCAOB established a research group, the Center for Economic Analysis. Board members of the PCAOB attend auditing research conferences (such as the American Accounting Association Auditing Section Midyear Meeting) and take part. CPA Australia also supports synthesis projects on Australian and New Zealand research (see for example Carson, Botica Redmayne, and Liao, 2014; Hay et al., 2017).[2]

Other recent examples of evidence-based investigations include the International Auditing and Assurance Board (IAASB)'s research projects conducted before introducing new audit reports, and a recent initiative by the International Ethics Standards Board for Accountants (IESBA) (Hay, 2017). The enhanced audit report is one area where auditors have recently innovated to meet the perceived needs of external users (Schilder, 2016). As discussed earlier, the IAASB made these changes after commissioning several research studies, which themselves used a mixture of methods from different disciplines. They included surveys, experiments, focus groups, and verbal protocol analysis in the US, UK, Germany, and New Zealand. The changes include the requirement for a much more extensive report, in which the auditor discusses Key Audit Matters that arose during the audit, so that stakeholders can be much more informed.

The IESBA project examined research that relates to ethical issues and that is concerned with audit fees. They considered research on four issues: fee level, dependence, non-audit fees, and firms that provide non-audit services. Although audit fee research does not convey a message that there are widespread ethical problems, there are some risk areas (Hay, 2017b). There is evidence that audit fees for new engagements are lower and that non-audit services affect independence in appearance. A few studies show that non-audit services provided by an auditor are associated with a loss of independence indicated by lower audit quality. There is concern about growth in non-audit services to non-audit clients, and there is some evidence that audit quality is lower when firms have more extensive non-audit services businesses.

The Office of the Auditor-General of New Zealand, commissioned research on "The Value of Public Auditing" (e.g., Cordery and Hay, 2016). Public sector auditing provides value, and in New Zealand there are innovative ways in which public sector auditors get feedback from stakeholders.

In Belgium, the Institute of Registered Auditors commissioned and published a study on the informativeness of extended audit reporting and the new KAM reporting for public interest entities (Gaeremynck, Willekens and De Wolf 2019).

There are further issues regarding barriers in transferring auditing research to standard setters (Hoang, Salterio, and Sylph, 2017). In disciplines where research is used extensively for evidence-based policy, there are well-established procedures for overcoming issues in transferring knowledge from researchers to standard setters (Hoang et al., 2017). Auditing and accounting researchers have yet to develop these techniques as effectively. Researchers can also influence the development of the auditing techniques used by audit firms. In the past, auditing researchers have claimed to have a productive collaboration with practitioners (Abdel-khalik and Solomon, 1988; Bell and Wright, 1995). More recently, there has been more focus on the needs of regulators.

These approaches may help, but there is also a fundamental problem: it is difficult for researchers to conduct meaningful research that will be useful in practice without access to audit firms and clients.

F Relevant audits for a wide range of stakeholders

Another fundamental issue in auditing is that of meeting the needs of stakeholders. Do auditors provide financial report users with what they want?

Recent changes have been notable in many countries, although the reforms (and current proposals) concentrate heavily on the needs of the users of the financial reports of large listed companies. Not all of the audits that are currently practiced are audits of large public listed companies, and not all financial report users are concerned with these large companies. Some of the research studies show that there are a wide range of others who rely on audit reports, in particular the users of financial statements of smaller organizations. The question might be asked: do the recent changes and current proposals benefit the users of small audits as well as large? There is some evidence that recent reforms do not fit the needs of these users very well (Millichamp and Taylor, 2018, 488; Jeffrey and Gambier, 2016, 5).

Voluntary audits and audits of smaller entities are another issue of wide concern. Much less is known about these audits; the regulations for them often differ, but there are nevertheless entities whose stakeholders require assurance (Vanstraelen and Schelleman, 2017). These smaller entities should not be neglected. Vanstraelen and Schelleman (2017) show that the issues regarding both demand for and supply of these audits are different, and that private companies are much more heterogeneous and have more firm-specific issues. There are research opportunities, and perhaps opportunities for new forms of assurance to be developed.

A related issue is that of developing ways to make auditing valuable in a wider range of settings: for example, environmental reporting, where auditing or assurance of environmental reports is becoming more widespread. Integrated reporting is an area where ideas about assurance being developed (Simnett, 2014). Auditing could also develop to meet user needs through different levels of assurance. Something less than a full-scale audit might be appropriate for smaller entities. Review engagements are an alternative in some circumstances. Some medium-sized charities in New Zealand are now required to have a review engagement, not an audit. Appropriate ways to provide assurance for small and medium enterprises is also being considered by standard setters.[3] More exploratory research is needed. Meeting the needs of a variety of users was also identified as needed by the ACCA/Grant Thornton working groups (Jeffrey and Gambier, 2016, 9).

More radically, perhaps "auditing" or similar activities can be distributed among non-experts in the community. Former Prime Minister of the United Kingdom David Cameron announced the abolition of the Audit Commission in 2009, and at the same time required local governments to provide more open data. His intention was that auditing of public sector expenditure could be crowdsourced to any individual who wishes to examine it (O'Leary, 2015). Cameron said, "Just imagine the effect that an army of armchair auditors is going to have on those expense claims" (O'Leary, 2015, 71). It is not yet clear whether there are armchair auditors, and what effect these people might have on expenditure. However, Susskind and Susskind (2015, 93) provide an example of grassroots individuals examining expenditure successfully, in the case of expenses claimed by Members of the UK Parliament.

G The partnership model

Why are audit firms usually operated as partnerships? One answer could be that there are economic reasons that make that form of entity more efficient.[4] Audit failures are rare, but have massive consequences, so that there need to be strong incentives for the audit team to be diligent and watchful for misstatements. Being a partner in charge of an audit is a great responsibility, and audit firms have developed their organization structure to protect the other partners (and incidentally, of course, the users of financial reports). The challenges of organizing highly skilled audit professionals to undertake this position of great responsibility are traditionally dealt with using the partnership model of audit firm organization. The partnership is a very old and very private form of business structure. It has been argued (Fama and Jensen, 1983) that retaining it for audit firms represents an economic response to the complex circumstances that auditors are in. There are a number of challenges that face audit firms as a business, including stiff competition, unlimited liability in some circumstances, and limited access to capital.

Someone who makes it to the level of partner in an audit firm is very carefully selected. The partnership provides a way of training and selecting the most suitable candidates from a large group of accounting graduates over a long time, so that their qualities are well known to an audit firm before they are selected. Audit firm partners are also highly rewarded in prestige and in financial terms, so that the audit firm can choose the potential partners that it finds most desirable. Fama and Jensen (1983) argue that the partnership model has the advantage that partners have a very strong incentive to monitor the quality of each other's work, because they are liable for losses resulting from errors by other partners in the firm. They argue that this economic reason, among others, is why partnerships are a successful economic response to the quality control issues.

However, this model is drawn from a period in which accounting firms, while large, were not as corporate and top-down as today's firms. Professional organizations (including universities, hospitals and many other entities as well as accounting and other professional firms) operated at the time under the "P2" (professional and partnership) model which gave individual professionals considerable autonomy and involvement in decisions affecting the whole firm (Greenwood, Hinings, and Brown, 1990). But an individual audit partner in Brussels, Orlando, or Auckland had little opportunity to control Arthur Andersen's choice of Enron as a client or the way in which the audit was conducted. The P2 model has now been superseded by more managerial models in accounting firms as well as in other sectors) (Cooper et al., 1996).

The special nature of audit firms compared to corporate entities is nevertheless important. Baskerville and Hay (2006) show that audit firms act in manner consistent with the partners acting in accordance with the incentive to maximize their own share of partnership net income – the firm does not maximize its overall revenue or net income. In another study, they showed that when a partnership is able to spread the risk over a larger group (a national firm, say, instead of a local city) then the partnership is able to accept clients that have a higher level of risk (Hay, Baskerville, and Qiu, 2007). The partnership model is thus an economic response to unusual features of auditing, and it can be seen to work. But much of the rest of the business world has moved to newer models of corporate governance. Audit partners are also now subject to much more formal controls by regulators and by their own firm networks inspecting their work. Given these changes, it may be that the partnership model will no longer be the best way to organize the providers of assurance services in the twenty-first century, or the preferred model for the future.

A study using unique data from Sweden examined the issue of partner income and audit quality (Knechel, Niemi, and Zerni, 2013, 352). The authors observed that a response to the European Commission's Green Paper on Audit Policy had commented that audit partner income was "more dependent on commercial incentives . . . than on audit quality." Their research found, among other results, that the size of an audit partner's personal client portfolio and acquisition of new clients are positively associated with the level of partner compensation.

Audit firms are increasingly being required to provide transparency reports,[5] and they provide more information than they have to, through press releases and other information. However, their transparency is still quite limited. Information about the people conducting the audits (their qualifications and experience or any past problems with their audits) might be relevant. Users of audit services might also expect to be able to find out about the management and ownership structures of audit firms, but this is usually not available. Where some information is available (e.g., for a US audit firm), it often shows a governance structure that is unusual compared to the usual corporate structure – particularly because it is all or nearly all made up of internal management, i.e., partners (see for example, KPMG, 2012). This seems surprising, and is unlikely to be the type of governance arrangement that the big firms would recommend for their own clients. There are many more stakeholders affected by the sound performance of an auditing firm than simply its owners, and it might be expected that considerable public information would be available, and that governance would be comparable to best practice for corporations.[6] Perhaps publishing a set of audited financial statements might be the most prominent concession to public accountability that would occur to a firm in the business of providing assurance on audited financial statements – but these are not available for most auditing firms.

A recent article (Wilson, 2017) cautioned the leaders of accounting firms that the partnership model, and the way some partners discuss it with their staff, were scaring away potential leaders. The dominance of the Big 4 is itself an issue that has been contentious in the past, and could well be again (Simunic, 1980; Millichamp and Taylor, 2018, 490).

H Predictions about the future of auditing

Predicting the future may remind you of bad science fiction. Where are the flying cars, hover boards, nuclear buses, or food in a pill that readers saw in the science fiction of the twentieth century? Suggestions about auditing in the future might look just as outlandish when we reflect on them some time in the future. But bold predictions of the future have not always been failures: consider mobile phones, tablet computers, flat screen TVs, or email. But taking into account those cautions, and those major trends, here is a picture of the future of auditing:

- Global: global influences will make a substantial difference, including greater longevity and the rise of newer economies
- Accounting will change; auditing therefore will also change
- Higher tech: information technology will be more influential, and auditing will need to learn to react more quickly to change
- Regulated: regulation of auditing and accounting will no longer be a matter of national sovereignty. It is in everyone's interest for auditing to be done well, and for there to be effective oversight of auditors. To avoid issues of conflicting national regulations, there needs to be a world body for auditing standards and oversight that is well accepted by all of the national government. Existing bodies such as IFAC, the IASB and the IAASB are not well-suited for such a role – although they take an international leadership role, they are fundamentally private bodies constituted by private national accounting institutes, although admittedly with structures to protect the public interest. In 2017, the Monitoring Group[7] released a consultation paper (The Monitoring Group, 2017). In its announcement it stated that "Removing the audit related standard setting activities from the profession and entering into a multi-stakeholder, geographically representative and independent governance structure would address concerns vis-á-vis the independence of standard setting." (Everts, 2017). There will be many difficulties in establishing such a body, setting its rules, and enforcing them. Differences in culture will cause continuing issues
- Research-based: more will be expected for auditors and audit firms to develop innovative auditing techniques. The current systems of auditing standards, inspection and liability encourages auditors to look backwards to what is generally accepted (Hay, 2017a)
- Relevant: auditing and assurance will need to become more diverse – with assurance for entities that need it, and not only for very large listed entities. That might mean other forms of assurance (or examination) at a lower level than the audit that a company such as Nokia in Finland or Fonterra in New Zealand requires. Relevant auditing might also be more diverse in covering internal control, environmental issues, privacy, and other issues that auditors have not yet considered. There is room for new kinds of assurance to give all kinds of user groups the assurance that they crave
- Re-structured: the partnership form is a reasonable economic approach to a very complex setting for a private sector business to operate in. But it will become much more open and accountable to be acceptable

as part of a future system of public accountability. It is possible to shine the light of modern corporate governance on audit firms or their future counterparts

Notes

1 In re: Kingston Cotton Mill Company (No. 2): "It is the duty of an auditor to bring to bear on the work he has to perform that skill, care, and caution which a reasonably competent, careful, and cautious auditor would use."
2 Another example is Sinclair and Cordery (2016).
3 www.ifac.org/global-knowledge-gateway/audit-assurance/what-future-assurance-and-small-business Accessed 14 November 2014.
4 Audit firms that are permitted to be constituted as corporations generally continue to use the partnership structure and terminology.
5 E.g., in Europe and Japan (International Organization of Securities Commissions, 2009) and in Australia (www.charteredaccountants.com.au/Industry-Topics/Audit-and-assurance/News-and-guidance-on-regulatory-matters/News-and-guidance-on-regulatory-matters/Audit-transparency-report-regulations-issued)
6 Audit firms recommend audit committees, and greater transparency, for other organizations – for example, www.pwc.com/gx/en/audit-services/publications/regulatory-debate/governance-transparency.jhtml.
7 The Monitoring Group consists of the International Organization of Securities Commissions (IOSCO), the Basel Committee on Banking Supervision, the European Commission, the Financial Stability Board, the International Association of Insurance Supervisors, the International Forum of Independent Audit Regulators, and the World Bank Group, and is chaired by IOSCO.

References

Abdel-khalik, A. R., and I. Solomon. 1988. *Research Opportunities in Auditing: The Second Decade*. Sarasota, FL: American Accounting Association: Auditing Section.

Accountancy Europe. 2017. *Follow-Up Paper: The Future of Corporate Reporting – Creating the Dynamics for Change*. Brussels: Accountancy Europe.

Alsaif, T. M., B. M. Savage, and D. M. Reed. 2018. Picking Low Hanging Fruit? Synergies Between Strategic Quality Management and Corporate Social Responsibility. *Business Process Management Journal* 24 (6): 1393–1411. doi:BPMJ-01-2018-0014

Anderson, A. W. 2017. *4 Keys to the Future of Audit*. https://tax.thomsonreuters.com/site/wp-content/private/pdf/checkpoint/whitepapers/Checkpoint-Al-Anderson-Whitepaper.pdf

Arrowsmith, R. 2018. Audit Dead in a Decade. *Accounting Today*. https://www.accountingtoday.com/news/audit-dead-in-a-decade

Bakker, P. 2013. Accountants Will Save the World. *Harvard Business Review*. https://hbr.org/2013/03/accountants-will-save-the-worl

Baskerville, R. F., and D. C. Hay. 2006. The Effect of Accounting Firm Mergers on the Market for Audit Services: New Zealand Evidence. *Abacus* 42 (1): 87–104.

Bedard, J. C., and L. Graham. 2014. Reporting on Internal Control. In *The Routledge Companion to Auditing*, edited by D. C. Hay, W. R. Knechel, and M. Willekens, 311–322. Abingdon, UK: Routldege.

Bell, T. B., and A. M. Wright. 1995. *Auditing Practice, Research, and Education: A Productive Collaboration.* New York, NY: American Institute of Certified Public Accountants.

Bradbury, M. E., and M. Almulla. 2018. Auditor, Client, and Investor Consequences of the Enhanced Auditor's Report. *SSRN Electronic Journal.* https://ssrn.com/abstract=3165267

Brown-Liburd, H., and M. A. Vasarhelyi. 2015, December. Big Data and Audit Evidence. *Journal of Emerging Technologies in Accounting* 12 (1): 1–16.

Byrnes, P. E., A. Al-Awadhi, B. Gullvist, H. Brown-liburd, R. Teeter, J. D. Warren, and M. Vasarhelyi. 2012. Evolution of Auditing: From the Traditional Approach to the Future Audit. *AICPA White Paper.* https://www.aicpa.org/interestareas/frc/assuranceadvisoryservices/downloadabledocuments/whitepaper_evolution-of-auditing.pdf

Canton, J., and Institute for Global Futures. 2015. *Welcome to the Fast Future . . .* New York, NY.: CPA.com.

Carson, E. 2014. Globalization of Auditing. In *The Routledge Companion to Auditing*, edited by D. C. Hay, W. R. Knechel, and M. Willekens, 23–32. Abingdon, UK: Routledge.

Carson, E., N. B. Redmayne, and L. Liao. 2014. Audit Market Structure and Competition in Australia. *Australian Accounting Review* 24 (4): 298–312.

Choi, J.-H., J.-B. Kim, X. Liu, and D. A. Simunic. 2008. Audit Pricing, Legal Liability Regimes, and Big 4 Premiums: Theory and Cross-Country Evidence. *Contemporary Accounting Research* 25 (1): 55–99.

Choudhury, F. 2014. It's Not Really About Bitcoin, It's About Change. *IFAC Global Knowledge Gateway.* file:///C:/Users/dhay026/Documents/data/audit/audit research/future of auditing/It's Not Really about Bitcoin, It's about Change _ IFAC.html

Chung, S., and R. Narasimhan. 2002. An International Study of Cross-Sectional Variations in Audit Fees. *International Journal of Auditing* 6 (1): 79–91.

Cohen, J. R., and W. R. Knechel. 2013. A Call for Academic Inquiry: Challenges and Opportunities from the PCAOB Synthesis Projects. *Auditing: A Journal of Practice & Theory* 32 (Supplement 1): 1–5.

Cooper, D. J., B. Hinings, R. Greenwood, J. L. Brown, D. J. Cooper, B. Hinings, R. Greenwood, and J. L. Brown. 1996. Sedimentation and Transformation in Organizational Change: The Case of Canadian Law Firms. *Organization Studies* 17 (4): 623–647.

Cordery, C. J., and D. C. Hay. 2016, September 6–8. Supreme Audit Institutions and Public Value: Demonstrating Relevance. In *9th International EIASM Public Sector Conference*, Lisbon, Portugal.

CPA Canada. 2013. *CPA Canada 2013 Shaping the Future of Audit Assurance.* www.cpacanada.ca/en/business-and-accounting-resources/audit-and-assurance/enhancing-audit-quality/publications/shaping-the-future-of-audit-assurance

Deloitte. 2016. *Audit of the Future Survey Results.* www2.deloitte.com/us/en/pages/audit/articles/the-future-of-audit-survey-and-innovation-report.html

Eierle, B., S. Hartlieb, D. C. Hay, L. Niemi, and H. Ojala. 2018. What Drives Differences in Audit Pricing Across the Globe? In *Second Scandinavian Accounting Research Conference.* Oslo.

Ellis, C. D. 2017. The End of Active Investing? *Financial Times*, January 20.

Everts, G. 2017. *Call for Comments on Reforms to the Global Audit Standard-Setting Process*. Madrid: The Monitoring Group.

Fama, E. F., and M. C. Jensen. 1983. Agency Problems and Residual Claims. *The Journal of Law and Economics* 26 (2): 327–349.

Fédération des Experts-comptables Européens. 2014. *The Future of Audit and Assurance*. Brussels.

———. 2016. *Pursuing a Strategic Debate*. Brussels.

Forbes. 2017. *Audit 2025 The Future is Now*. Jersey City, NJ.

Forbes Insight. 2015. *Future Role of Audit a More Insightful Audit for a More Complex World*. 1–14.

Francis, J. R. 2011. Auditing Without Borders. *Accounting, Organizations and Society* 36 (4–5): 318–323.

Francis, J. R., P. N. Michas, and S. E. Seavey. 2013. Does Audit Market Concentration Harm the Quality of Audited Earnings? Evidence From Audit Markets in 42 Countries. *Contemporary Accounting Research* 30 (1): 325–355.

Francis, J. R., and D. Wang. 2008. The Joint Effect of Investor Protection and Big 4 Audits on Earnings Quality Around the World. *Contemporary Accounting Research* 25 (1): 157–191.

Gaeremynck, A., M. Willekens;, and M. De Wolf. 2019. *Key Audit Matters (KAM) - Points clés de l'audit - Kernpunten van de Controle*. Ed. ICCI. Antwerpen: Maklu.

Gay, G. E., and R. Simnett. 2015. *Auditing and Assurance Services in Australia*. 6th ed. North Ryde: McGraw-Hill Education (Australia).

Greenwood, R., C. R. Hinings, and J. Brown. 1990. "P2-Form" Strategic Management: Corporate Practices in Professional Partnerships. *Academy of Management Journal* 33 (4): 725–755.

Gutierrez, E., M. Minutti-Meza, K. W. Tatum, and M. Vulcheva. 2018. Consequences of Adopting an Expanded Auditor's Report in the United Kingdom. *Review of Accounting Studies* 23 (4): 1543–1587.

Hanes, D. R., B. M. Porco, and J. C. Thibodeau. 2014. Simply Soups Inc.: A Teaching Case Designed to Integrate the Electronic Cash Confirmation Process Into the Auditing Curriculum. *Issues in Accounting Education* 29 (2): 349–358.

Harris, S. 2017. Technology and the Audit of Today and Tomorrow. In *PCAOB/AAA Annual Meeting*. Washington, DC: PCAOB.

Hay, D. C. 2017a. Opportunities for Auditing Research: Back to Our Interdisciplinary Roots. Ed. C. de Villiers and C. de Villiers. *Meditari Accountancy Research* 25 (3): 336–350.

———. 2017b. Audit Fee Research on Issues Related to Ethics. *Current Issues in Auditing*, 11 (2): A1–A22. doi: 10.2308/ciia-51897

Hay, D. C., R. F. Baskerville, and T. H. Qiu. 2007. The Association Between Partnership Financial Integration and Risky Audit Client Portfolios. *Auditing: A Journal of Practice & Theory* 26 (2): 57–68.

Hay, D. C., J. Stewart, and N. Botica Redmayne. 2017. The Role of Auditing in Corporate Governance in Australia and New Zealand: A Research Synthesis. *Australian Accounting Review* 27 (4): 457–479.

Hill, K. 2011. So, What Are These Privacy Audits That Google and Facebook Have to Do for the Next 20 Years? *Forbes*. www.forbes.com/sites/kashmirhill/2011/11/30/

so-what-are-these-privacy-audits-that-google-and-facebook-have-to-do-for-the-next-20-years/.

Hoang, K. J., S. E. Salterio, and J. Sylph. 2017. Barriers to Transferring Accounting and Auditing Research to Standard Setters. Working paper available at https://papers.ssrn.com/sol3/papers.cfm?abstract_id=2928450

Holderness, D. K. 2014. Continuous Auditing. In *The Routledge Companion to Auditing*, edited by D. C. Hay, W. R. Knechel, and M. Willekens. Abingdon, UK: Routledge.

Humphrey, C., A. Loft, and A. Samsonova-Taddei. 2014. Not Just a Standard Story: The Rise of International Standards on Auditing. In *The Routledge Companion to Auditing*, edited by D. C. Hay, W. R. Knechel, and M. Willekens, 161–178. Abingdon, UK: Routledge.

IAASB. 2013a. *A Framework for Audit Quality: Discussion Paper*. New York, NY: IAASB.

———. 2013b. *At a Glance: Consultation Paper, Audit Quality*. New York, NY: IAASB.

———. 2014. *A Framework for Audit Quality*. New York, NY: IAASB.

———. 2015. *Auditor Reporting*. www.iaasb.org/projects/auditor-reporting

IAASB Data Analytics Working Group. 2016. *Exploring the Growing Use of Technology in the Audit, With a Focus on Data Analytics*. New York, NY: IAASB Data Analytics Working Group.

ICAEW. 2017. *Artificial Intelligence and the Future of Accountancy*. London: ICAEW.

———. 2018. The Future of Audit: Technology. *Technical Resources*. www.icaew.com/en/technical/audit-and-assurance/faculty/the-future-of-audit/the-future-of-audit-technology

IIRC. 2014. *Assurance on IR: An Introduction to the Discussion*. London: International Integrated Reporting Council. http://integratedreporting.org/wp-content/uploads/2014/07/Assurance-on-IR-an-introduction-to-the-discussion.pdf

International Auditing and Assurance Standards Board. 2012. *Invitation to Comment: Improving the Auditor's Report*. New York, NY: International Auditing and Assurance Standards Board.

International Forum of Independent Audit Regulators. 2018. *About IFIAR*. www.ifiar.org/about/

International Organization of Securities Commissions. 2009. *Transparency of Firms that Audit Public Companies. Consultation Report, Technical Committee of the International Organization of Securities Commissions*. Madrid: International Organization of Securities Commissions.

Jaggi, B. L., and P. Y. Low. 2011. Joint Effect of Investor Protection and Securities Regulations on Audit Fees. *International Journal of Accounting* 46 (3): 241–270.

Jeffrey, N., and A. Gambier. 2016. *The Future of Audit*. London: ACCA.

Karapetrovic, S., and W. Willborn. 2002. Self-Audit of Process Performance. *International Journal of Quality and Reliability Management* 19 (1): 24–45.

Knechel, W. R. 2013. Do Auditing Standards Matter? *Current Issues in Auditing* 7 (2): A1–A16.

———. 2016. Audit Quality and Regulation. *International Journal of Auditing* 20 (3): 215–223.

Knechel, W. R., N. Mintchik, M. Pevzner, and U. Velury. 2018. The Effects of Generalized Trust and Civic Cooperation on the Big N Presence and Audit Fees

Across the Globe. *Auditing: A Journal of Practice & Theory* 38 (1): 193–219. Forthcoming.

Knechel, W. R., L. Niemi, and M. Zerni. 2013. Empirical Evidence on the Implicit Determinants of Compensation in Big 4 Audit Partnerships. *Journal of Accounting Research* 51 (2): 349–387.

Kontis, V., J. E. Bennett, C. D. Mathers, G. Li, K. Foreman, and M. Ezzati. 2017. Future Life Expectancy in 35 Industrialised Countries: Projections With a Bayesian Model Ensemble. *The Lancet* 389 (10076): 1323–1335.

KPMG. 2012. *International Annual Review*. https://home.kpmg/content/dam/kpmg/pdf/2013/12/kpmg-international-annual-review-2012.pdf

KPMG International. 2013. *Future State 2030: The Global Megatrends Shaping Governments*. https://assets.kpmg/content/dam/kpmg/pdf/2014/02/future-state-2030-v3.pdf

Lamoreaux, P. T., P. N. Michas, and W. L. Schultz. 2015. Do Accounting and Audit Quality Affect World Bank Lending? *The Accounting Review* 90 (2): 703–738.

Lennox, C. S., J. J. Schmidt, and A. Thompson. 2015. Is the Expanded Model of Audit Reporting Informative to Investors? Evidence From the UK. *SSRN*. https://ssrn.com/abstract=2619785

Li, H., D. Hay, and D. Lau. 2019. Assessing the impact of the new auditor's report. *Pacific Accounting Review* 31 (1): 110–132.

Liebes, T., and Z. Kampf. 2009. The Changing Relationships Among Media, Government, and Public: The Case of War. *The Communication Review* 12 (3): 195–198.

Maestas, N., and J. Zissimopoulos. 2010. How Longer Work Lives Ease the Crunch of Population Aging. *Journal of Economic Perspectives* 24 (1): 139–160.

Malmgren, P. 2017. New World Audit. *Acuity*, 26–31.

Maltby, J. 2009. Auditing. In *The Routledge Companion to Accounting History*, edited by J. R. Edwards, and S. P. Walker, 224–244. Abingdon, UK: Routledge.

Marriage, M. 2017. *Technology Takes the Tedium Out of Auditing*. www.ft.com/content/a58b4b42-9ec8-11e7-9a86-4d5a475ba4c5

Michas, P. N. 2011. The Importance of Audit Profession Development in Emerging Market Countries. *The Accounting Review* 86 (5): 1731–1764.

Millichamp, A., and J. Taylor. 2018. *Auditing*. 11th ed. Andover, UK: Cengage.

Mock, T. J., J. L. Turner, G. L. Gray, and P. Coram. 2009. The Unqualified Auditor's Report: A Study of User Perceptions, Effects on User Decisions and Decision Processes, and Directions for Further Research. *A Report to the ASB and IAASB*, 24.

Modigliani, F., and R. Brumberg. 1955. Utility Analysis and the Consumption Function: An Interpretation of Cross-Section Data. In *Post Keynesian Economics*, edited by K. K. Kurihara, 388–436. London: Routledge.

The Monitoring Group. 2017. *Monitoring Group Consultation: Strengthening the Governance and Oversight of the International Audit-Related Standard-Setting Boards in the Public Interest*. Madrid. https://www.iosco.org/library/pubdocs/pdf/IOSCOPD586.pdf

Murphy, H. 2017. Auditing to be Less of a Burden as Accountants Embrace AI. *Financial Times*. www.ft.com/content/0898ce46-8d6a-11e7-a352-e46f43c5825d.

Nakashima, M., and D. A. Ziebart. 2015. Did Japanese-SOX Have an Impact on Earnings Management and Earnings Quality? *Managerial Auditing Journal* 30 (4–5): 482–510.

Nikkinen, J., and P. Sahlström. 2004. Does Agency Theory Provide a General Framework for Audit Pricing? *International Journal of Auditing* 8 (3): 253–262.

Offermans, M., and A. Vanstraelen. 2014. Oversight and Inspection of Auditing. In *The Routledge Companion to Auditing*, edited by D. C. Hay, W. R. Knechel, and M. Willekens, 179–188. Abingdon, UK: Routledge.

O'Leary, D. E. 2015. Armchair Auditors: Crowdsourcing Analysis of Government Expenditures. *Journal of Emerging Technologies in Accounting* 12 (1): 71–91.

Organization for Economic Cooperation and Development (OECD). 2013. *Education at a Glance 2013*. Education at a Glance. Geneva: OECD Publishing.

Percy, J. P. 1999. Assurance Services: Visions for the Future. *International Journal of Auditing* 3 (2): 81–87.

Porter, B. 2014. The Audit Expectationgap: A Persistent But Changing Phenomenon. In *The Routledge Companion to Auditing*, edited by D. C. Hay, W. R. Knechel, and M. Willekens, 43–53. Abingdon, UK: Routledge.

Porter, B., C. Ó Hógartaigh, and R. F. Baskerville. 2012. Audit Expectation-Performance Gap Revisited: Evidence From New Zealand and the United Kingdom. Part 2: Changes in the Gap in New Zealand 1989–2008 and in the United Kingdom 1999–2008. *International Journal of Auditing* 16 (3): 215–247.

Posner, C. 2017. The CAMs are Coming: PCAOB Adopts New Standard to Enhance Audit Reports. *Cooley PubCo Blog*. https://cooleypubco.com/2017/06/02/the-cams-are-coming-pcaob-adopts-new-standard-to-enhance-audit-reports/

Public Company Accounting Oversight Board. 2017. PCAOB Adopts New Standard to Enhance the Relevance and Usefulness of the Auditor's Report With Additional Information for Investors. *News Release*. Washington, DC: PCAOB. https://pcaobus.org/News/Releases/Pages/auditors-report-standard-adoption-6-1-17.aspx

PwC. 2012. *Initial Assessment Report on Google's Privacy Program*. https://epic.org/privacy/ftc/googlebuzz/FTC-Initial-Assessment-09-26-12.pdf

———. 2018. *Financial Statement Audit: Tech-Enabling the Audit for Enhanced Quality and Greater Insights*. www.pwc.com/us/audit?WT.mc_id=CT1-PL50-DM1-TR1-LS3-ND30-TTA4-CN_AuditInnovation-&eq=CT1-PL50-DM1-CN_AuditInnovation

Raj, V. 2017. *Will External Audits Vanish in the Blockchain World*. www.ifac.org/global-knowledge-gateway/audit-assurance/discussion/will-external-audits-vanish-blockchain-world

Rapoport, M., and B. Dummett. 2012. U.S. Sues Big Firms Over China Audits. *The Wall Street Journal*. www.wsj.com/articles/SB10001424127887324355904578157252180759338.

Reid, L. C., J. V. Carcello, C. Li, and T. L. Neal. 2018, July 11. Impact of Auditor Report Changes on Financial Reporting Quality and Audit Costs: Evidence From the United Kingdom. *Contemporary Accounting Research*. Forthcoming.

Reuters Staff. 2017. Timeline: US, HK Regulators Struggle to Get China Audit Papers. *Reuters Business News*. www.reuters.com/article/china-audit-timeline/timeline-u-s-hk-regulators-struggle-to-get-china-audit-papers-idUSKBN1EE0HT

Rowland, M. 2018. The Evolution of Audit. *CA Today*. www.icas.com/ca-today-news/the-evolution-of-audit

Schilder, A. 2016. The Future of Audit. In *ACCA-Grant Thornton Future of Audit Conference*, 2. Brussels.

Shimamoto, D. C. 2018. Why Accountants Must Embrace Machine Learning. *Global Knowledge Gateway*. http://www.ifac.org/global-knowledge-gateway/technology/discussion/why-accountants-must-embrace-machine-learning?utm_medium=social&utm_source=email&utm_campaign=web_share#.Wpby35Q1ReM.email

Simnett, R. 2014. Assurance of Environment, Social and Sustainability Information. In *The Routledge Companion to Auditing*, edited by D. C. Hay, W. R. Knechel, and M. Willekens, 325–337. Abingdon, UK: Routldege.

Simunic, D. A. 1980. The Pricing of Audit Services: Theory and Evidence. *Journal of Accounting Research* 18 (1): 161.

Sinclair, R., and C. J. Cordery. 2016. Bridging the Gap Between Academia and Industry. *Pacific Accounting Review* 28 (2): 135–152.

Srinidhi, B. N., M. Hossain, and C. Y. Lim. 2012. The Effect of Arthur Andersen's Demise on Clients' Audit Fees and Auditor Conservatism: International Evidence. *Journal of International Financial Management and Accounting* 23 (3): 208–244.

Susskind, R., and D. Susskind. 2015. *The Future of the Professions*. Ebook. Oxford: Oxford University Press.

Taylor, M. H., and D. T. Simon. 1999. Determinants of Audit Fees: The Importance of Litigation, Disclosure, and Regulatory Burdens in Audit Engagements in 20 Countries. *The International Journal of Accounting* 34 (3): 375–388.

Thompson, P. 2017. Digital Technologies' Implications for SMPs. *IFAC Global Knowledge Gateway*. www.ifac.org/global-knowledge-gateway/practice-management/discussion/digital-technologies-implications-smps.

Toy, A., and D. C. Hay. 2015. Privacy Auditing Standards. *Auditing: A Journal of Practice & Theory* 34 (3): 181–199.

Van Linden, C., and T. Mazza. 2018. Quality Control System Criticism Raised by the Public Company Accounting Oversight Board in Non-US Jurisdictions and Earnings Quality of Non-Cross-Listed Clients. *International Journal of Auditing* 22 (3): 374–384.

Vanstraelen, A., and C. Schelleman. 2017. Auditing Private Companies: What do We Know? *Accounting and Business Research* 47 (5): 565–584.

Walton, M. 2010, September. Investigative Shortfall. *American Journalism Review*, 18–30.

Wammes, B. 2016. Accountants Are Going to Save the World. *IFAC Global Knowledge Gateway*. www.ifac.org/global-knowledge-gateway/viewpoints/accountants-are-going-save-world.

Wang, L., Q. Xu, and J. Zeng. 2014. *China SOX, Dual Auditing Firms and Financial Restatements*. Working Paper. Hong Kong: Hong Kong Polytechnic University.

Wilson, J. 2017. Stop Scaring Away Your Future Leaders. *Journal of Accountancy*. file:///C:/Users/dhay026/Documents/Data/Audit/Audit Research/Future of Auditing/Stop Scaring Away Your Future Leaders. *Journal of Accountancy*.html.

World Bank Group. 2015. *Purchasing Power Parities and the Real Size of World Economies*. Washington, DC: World Bank Group.

Zhou, S., R. Simnett, and H. Hoang. 2018. Evaluating Combined Assurance as a New Credibility Enhancement Technique. *Auditing: A Journal of Practice & Theory* forthcoming, doi: 10.2308/ajpt-52175

4 Opportunities for auditing research

Auditing is a professional, economic, and regulated activity executed by individuals with the help of audit technology. These interrelated aspects of auditing provide opportunities for research. Audits and the audit market are very heavily regulated. Who needs an audit, who can supply an audit, and the conditions under which the two parties can contract for audit services are all subject to various forms of regulation. There is also a risk of litigation against the auditor in case of malpractice. The past decade has seen a large increase, globally, in regulation of auditing and auditors.

The technology of accounting and auditing are changing, and some observers perceive threats to professions like accounting and auditing (Susskind and Susskind, 2015). Given all these aspects, auditing is a complex phenomenon to study and understand. Over the past 30 years, audit research has grown exponentially and researchers have learned a tremendous amount about auditing, auditors, and audit markets. In this section, which draws on chapter 28 of *The Routledge Companion to Auditing* (Hay, Knechel, and Willekens, 2014), I reflect on some key issues for future research and discuss more recent developments.

A Audit quality

Audit quality is a key concern for auditors, regulators, and users of financial information. A lot of previous research has examined the question of audit quality. Yet the auditing community still has little understanding of what audit quality means, and there is no consensus as to what constitutes it (Knechel and Shefchik, 2014; Cahan, 2014). What constitutes audit quality for one stakeholder may not do so for another. Audit quality research remains a useful and fertile research domain. Hence, a topic for future research is to investigate what constitutes audit value and/or quality for different stakeholders and in different institutional settings.

Various definitions of audit quality have been advanced, as discussed by Knechel and Shefchik (2014), from the traditional DeAngelo (1981) approach based on the combination of auditor independence and competence, to audit quality defined as the amount of work performed by the auditor. Numerous empirical audit quality studies define audit quality in terms of a financial statement outcome, e.g., an auditor's ability to constrain earnings management (see Cahan, 2014). While earnings management measures are widely used, they are also widely accepted to be a very limited measure of audit quality that is used only because better alternatives are often not available. Further development in this area has included consideration of models of the audit process that take account of inputs, the process, and outputs (Knechel, Krishnan, Pevzner, Shefchik, and Velury, 2013; IAASB, 2013). The IAASB Framework for Audit Quality adopted in 2014 incorporates inputs, processes, and outputs (IAASB, 2014).

The paper by Knechel, Krishnan, Pevzner, Shefchik, and Velury (2013) and the IAASB Framework (IAASB, 2014) were a substantial step forward in auditing quality. Researchers now need to consider adopting more of their elements. Future research could address how the primary attributes of an audit affect different indicators of audit quality. Another useful area could be to study the links between the different indicators of audit quality. Furthermore, development of new metrics for measuring audit quality beyond those borrowed from financial accounting research seems necessary and warranted.

B Independence

Auditor independence continues to attract significant interest from stakeholders, regulators, policy makers, and the audit profession itself. Auditor independence rules have become stricter. Nevertheless, there is very little causal evidence that auditor characteristics, such as long tenure or the provision of non-audit services (NAS), impair independence. Research that investigates auditor independence typically tests the association between an auditor characteristic (such as tenure or joint NAS supply) and a financial statement or auditor-based dependent variable (such as earnings management or the likelihood of a going concern opinion). When, on rare occasions, a significant association is found, it is then attributed to the presence of an auditor independence problem. However, associations between auditor characteristics and quality measures could equally be attributable to competence. For example, when no significant association between tenure and earnings management is found, this could be due to the fact that independence and competence are not readily separable, or that they have opposite effects.

Research so far has only provided circumstantial evidence about auditor independence, as Sharma (2014) points out. Causal links between specific auditor/auditee attributes and audit quality are difficult to prove. Nevertheless, standard setters are taking a keen interest, and research that explores the issue has been followed by, for example, the International Ethics Standards Board for Accountants (Hay, 2018b). Clever research designs that enable demonstration of a causal relationship between certain auditor attributes and audit quality would be a welcome addition to auditing research. Recent concerns about this issue include the growth in non-audit services to non-audit clients, which some regulators and researchers see as a danger to the integrity of audit firms (Dey, Robin, and Tessoni, 2012; United States Treasury, 2008).

Radical proposals including restricting audit firms to audit services only (Francis, 2004), or requiring the Big 4 firms to break up into smaller entities (Jones, 2018; Marriage, 2018) are discussed from time to time. Independence, and its related issues, will continue to be an important topic.

C Regulation

Auditing is a highly regulated activity, and considerable new regulation has arisen during the last decade. As auditing has become a global activity, regulatory concerns have also expanded (Carson, 2014). The global financial crisis demonstrated the interconnectedness of the global economy, particularly in relation to the tightness of credit markets. However, there is little global regulatory oversight of the activities of global firm networks despite the existence of International Standards on Auditing. Future research could address the issue of the extent to which audit quality differs across countries and regulatory settings, and why.

Another area of potential research relates to the audit of multinationals and of cross-border transactions. An area of major change in regulation is oversight and inspection – see Offermans and Vanstraelen (2014). So far, research on the effects of oversight and inspection mainly stems from US experience. With the introduction of various forms of inspection around the world, future research should examine the differing effects of different approaches. In addition, we know very little about the efficiency and effectiveness of different forms of public oversight, and so more research on that topic would be valuable. Another question is the differences between inspection regimes that disclose or do not disclose outcomes to the public.

It would also be valuable to learn more about the implications of changes in the audit process brought about by inspections of auditors' work. To what extent do audit firms learn about inspection processes and likely inspection targets? Recently there has been a lengthy debate about whether auditor reporting is appropriate and sufficient.

Many believe that auditors do not provide the investing public with enough of an insight into the quality of a company's financial reporting, and, especially, have not provided adequate warning of impending business failures. Standard setters recently considered changes in the auditor's reporting responsibilities, including reconsideration of how an auditor should address issues related to a client who may have significant going concern uncertainties (Coram, 2014; Geiger, 2014). Going concern is a recurring issue that has not been resolved yet, and will need to be revisited.

A new issue in the discussion of standards is the new requirements for auditors to disclose key audit issues (key audit matters or critical audit matters) in their report, an area where there is still only limited research. Future research could address the question of whether the changes in auditor reporting do indeed affect stakeholder decisions.

D Audit markets

Auditing is an economic activity that takes place in a market. Little is known so far about audit market segmentation and the way auditors compete in the audit market. Research about cost minimization strategies of auditors is virtually non-existent due to lack of auditor cost data. However, such studies could add tremendously to our understanding of the drivers of audit quality.

Various studies have investigated the effects of industry specialization on audit pricing and quality. However, an auditor differentiation strategy can be defined in many ways. As Jeter states (2014), specialization could be defined in a variety of ways, such as specialization in particular income statement or balance sheet accounts (e.g., valuation of intangibles) or in specific aspects of the audit engagement (e.g., accounting for mergers). Furthermore, the way industry specialization is measured in prior research is subject to limitations, as most studies use proxies based on market share, which may actually capture the market power an auditor has in the market segment rather than the firm's level of expertise. Hence, future research that addresses the effects on quality, pricing, and competition of auditor differentiation beyond industry specialization would be very valuable. Auditor specialization is an area of research that appears to be reaching limits of its usefulness. The existence of conflicting results and inconsistent measures (Minutti-Meza, 2013; Audousset-Coulier, Jeny, and Jiang, 2016) suggest that there has been a lot of effort devoted to this area of research with very little overall increase in our knowledge. Fresh approaches are needed.

Cross-border regulation is already an important issue, and increased trends towards globalization and the rise of trade wars make it even more topical. It appears that the world is a long way from having global regulation and oversight of auditing, but that will be necessary for a seamless international investment market to exist.

E Auditing and governance

An external audit can be seen as an aspect within the broader set of governance tools that a company has established to assure reliable financial reporting, among other objectives. Other important governance mechanisms in this setting are internal control over financial reporting, internal auditing, and the board of directors, especially the audit committee. Ineffective internal control systems have been recognized as a major factor in facilitating large-scale frauds and erroneous financial reporting, and during the past decade, major regulatory changes have been imposed in some jurisdictions with respect to internal control reporting both by directors and auditors. A key issue is attaining the right balance of benefits versus costs of internal controls through legislation and regulation. As Bedard and Graham (2014) state, the research community is still finding its way in this new era, and while some evidence suggests that increased attention to internal controls has resulted in improvements in financial reporting, research should continue to investigate the association over time.

Studies that address the effects of variations in regulations across countries may provide insight as to the optimal balance of benefits and costs of compliance. A major challenge, however, is to define a research design that controls for related differences in other institutional factors. Internal auditing is also an important monitoring mechanism in many companies, and the audit profession could benefit from insights with respect to the internal audit function's role in enterprise risk management (ERM), compliance and combined assurance, as well as for external audit resource allocation and planning. Research on this topic could also inform practitioners and standard setters on ways to improve organizational governance (Anderson and Christ, 2014). Finally, the audit committee is assigned the task of overseeing the company's relations with the external auditor and safeguarding auditor independence. As such, it contributes to ensuring the quality of the external audit and reinforces confidence in the auditor's report. As Bédard and Compernolle (2014) state, future research could address how well audit committees assume their roles, as regulators seem to rely on the audit committee by increasing their responsibilities. Prior studies have highlighted the important influence of the processes, relationships, and communications among the audit committee, the auditor, and management on the audit committee's oversight of the external audit. Further research is required to better understand how the audit committee plays its oversight role in practice. This is an area where qualitative research will probably be the most effective approach.

Whether audit committees are able to respond to regulators' and the public's expectations is an unanswered empirical question. As audit committees are only one piece in the corporate governance mosaic, future research on the interaction among the various pieces of governance would also be worthwhile.

Corporate governance is an area of research that is of considerable interest in many disciplinary areas. What constitutes good corporate governance, and how that affects performance, are interesting to managers as well as to auditors. It is not yet clear whether good governance is associated with good performance. Examining that question is made more complicated by causality issues. The companies with the best governance are likely to be companies that are overcoming performance problems by bringing in better governance mechanisms. In that case, tests of statistical relationships are likely to find that better governance is associated with worse performance. As a result, it is not surprising that there is no strong evidence that good governance is effective. There are opportunities for research that builds on work from other disciplines. There is likely to be unexplored demand from directors and other people charged with governance for research studies that help them to know what corporate governance mechanisms work best. At present, much of the evidence is still equivocal (Hay, Stewart, and Botica Redmayne, 2017).

Corporate governance and internal control are issues of interest from a more specific auditing point of view. Bédard and Compernolle (2014) show that management continues to have some influence over the auditor, even when the audit committee is formally responsible for the auditor's appointment and remuneration. What we know about internal control has expanded considerably in the last decade because US companies and their auditors are required to disclose information about internal control weaknesses. Weaknesses are associated with company failure, and there is a share price reaction (Doyle et al., 2007). In the US, the requirements of SOX appear to be well-accepted. Other countries, namely Japan and China, have adopted some equivalent of SOX. However, this is not the case in Europe, Australia, New Zealand, or South Africa. These differences are an opportunity for researchers because they create opportunities to examine the costs and benefits of auditors reporting on internal control.

F Auditing in private companies and other settings

In many countries, auditing is not only mandatory for publicly listed companies due to securities laws (as in the US and Australia), it is also mandatory for many private companies due to an audit requirement in company laws (as in Europe). Research on auditing in private companies has so far mostly chosen topics that have previously been analyzed for public companies. However, as Langli and Svanstrom (2014) point out, it is possible to further advance the literature by asking questions that are more relevant for private companies and also to conduct tests that are not feasible in a public company setting. Research in Europe is making advances in this area. There are opportunities for research in the rest of the world, especially in countries that are not often examined.

G Under-researched auditing research areas

1 Replications

Replications of previous studies are not conducted frequently in auditing research. Replications and extensions of previous research studies ought to be conducted more often, and it should be possible for papers using such an approach to be accepted by journals. Increased use of repeated examinations of data through replications also allows for the knowledge from successive studies to be accumulated through meta-analysis and other systematic reviews. The use of meta-analysis in auditing is growing (Khlif and Chalmers, 2015), but there is still room for it to develop further (Hay, 2018a). Research of this type needs to show careful examination of the setting, and explanation in detail, perhaps using case vignettes.

2 Innovative settings

At the other extreme of the spectrum of research choices, there is also a need for research that closely examines auditing in innovative settings. Internationally, audit research is expanding, and in some cases, there are settings or data that allow important questions to be examined. More international research on international issues is also needed. Other countries that are already widely researched also provide opportunities: for example, in New Zealand, South Africa, Australia, the UK, and European countries. New sources of data are becoming available, such as in China.

Auditing research journals do not often publish research about emerging economies (Stewart, 2014). Considering the importance placed on auditing in developing countries by entities like the World Bank, this is surprising. It can be difficult to conduct research in such settings. Research questions need to be relevant to the international auditing community, preferably taking advantage of unique features of their setting, and to maintain high quality. Conducting research about auditing in developing economies is an opportunity for auditing researchers to make a difference to the world economy. Research that takes advantage of this opportunity should be based on the unique features of the country or setting being examined, rather than attempting to follow research in large country settings very closely. There are substantial opportunities for this type of research.

3 Auditing ethics

Although ethics are at the heart of the demand for auditing, the topic remains an under-researched area. As Shaub and Braun (2014) state, the current issues in ethics are largely unchanged from what they were prior to SOX (the Sarbanes-Oxley Act of 2002) or even what they were in the 1980s. This offers much research potential for the future, especially in investigating the link between individual auditor ethics characteristics and audit quality issues. Shaub and Braun (2014) also show that while auditing research raises many ethical issues, the researchers do not usually examine them. While this deficiency has unfortunate consequences, it also implies that opportunities exist.

4 Expectation gap

The expectation gap is a widely recognized and experienced phenomenon, but research in this area is mainly limited to two countries, namely the UK and New Zealand (Porter, 2014). That suggests that there is an opportunity to explore evidence about the expectation gap in other settings. Research about the link between the size and composition of the expectation gap and the institutional setting where it is observed seem worthwhile topics for future research. Other research in this area could relate to the consequences of variations in the expectation gap across countries. It may be that more sophisticated techniques of research than the current survey methodologies can be used.

In addition, auditing standards have changed, especially since the time when the early expectation-gap research was carried out. The changes reflect awareness of the existence of the expectation gap, and are often a response to the deficient standards gap, and sometimes to deficient performance or unreasonable expectations. Exploring the changes, and how they relate to the expectation gap, is an area with potential, and so is using the gap areas to predict future changes.

5 New forms of assurance

Assurance has gone through significant changes over the past two decades, mainly with respect to two dimensions. First, assurance has moved beyond financial statement assurance alone. Second, an evolution has taken place with regard to techniques of assurance. Simnett (2014) discusses research with respect to assurance of publicly available environmental, social, and sustainability reports. Research on assurance in these areas is still in its infancy, which offers tremendous potential for valuable future research. For example, future research could investigate competition in this segment of the assurance market, which is mostly unregulated. It could examine the effect of these new assurance services on competition, pricing, and quality in the financial statement assurance market.

Continuous auditing can also be seen as a new form of assurance. Holderness (2014) notes that the rate of adoption of continuous auditing lags considerably behind the technological capabilities for it. Continuous auditing has been on the agenda for some time (Byrnes et al., 2012). A domain for potential research is the reasons for such a lag. As the use of continuous auditing by external auditors lags behind that of internal auditors, studying continuous auditing in internal auditing settings may be a worthwhile avenue for future research from which the external audit profession could learn. Another interesting approach could be to examine the circumstances under which the reliance on transactional analysis (which is typically done in continuous auditing) on a more frequent basis throughout the year leads to an improvement in overall audit quality.

There are a wide range of other assurance areas including privacy, integrated reporting, and quality auditing. There are corresponding auditing research opportunities.

6 Fraud research

Carpenter and Austin (2014) argue that the public does not fully understand the auditor's responsibility for fraud or the rarity of its occurrence, creating an expectation gap between the audit profession and the public. Improving auditors' fraud detection skills is a significant challenge for the accounting profession, and the audit research community could help by studying fraud situations and contexts. However, just as fraud detection is challenging for auditors, so is fraud research for researchers. One major reason is lack of sufficient data. Carpenter and Austin (2014) suggest that researchers, policymakers, and auditors should work together to study this important topic, and disentangle risky fraud situations and incentives, to develop effective measures against fraud. One important question to answer is whether the systematic use of forensic specialists is cost effective, given the relatively low base rate of actual fraud. They further suggest that those interested in fraud detection research should consider work in related disciplines such as criminal justice, psychology, and organizational behavior.

There is now increasing interest in fraud education (Kranacher, Morris, Pearson, and Riley, 2008). Growth in this area might also encourage researchers to consider fraud research questions and how to examine them.

7 Judgment research

Another area for future research is the judgments made by auditors. As Trotman (2014) points out, the entire process of auditing is permeated by professional judgment. Today, more than ever, the profession finds itself face-to-face with numerous challenging and complex judgments. Hence, judgment research is and will continue to be a crucial research domain that will contribute to our understanding of the determinants of audit quality. Examples of auditor-related judgments that require deeper investigation include evaluating fair value and other estimates, professional skepticism, the use of analytical procedures, audit sampling, the effect of clients' use of service organizations, the degree of reliance on the internal audit function, and the audit report decision. Judgment research is part of the domain of psychology, where there is an ongoing crisis over whether well-known studies stand up to attempts to replicate them (Open Science Collaboration, 2015; Maxwell, Lau, and Howard, 2015). There is potential for researchers to re-examine existing auditor judgment research, and report on whether the results are reproducible.

The judgment side of auditing also has an ethical dimension, and this in itself opens up a large avenue for future research. As Shaub and Braun illustrate (Shaub and Braun, 2014), every major auditor choice issue being studied has an ethical component that is largely ignored. Recognizing and dealing with this flaw in our research designs may tremendously advance our knowledge about auditor decision making.

H Unresolved issues requiring future research

Audit failures of the twenty-first century have led some to believe that auditing is in a state of crisis, and further radical reforms are required. Indeed, this is usually the case, and some "current" issues have persisted for more than 100 years (Chandler and Edwards, 1996).

At a time when more regulation of various kinds is heavily on the agenda, it would be helpful to know a lot more about the settings and circumstances in which voluntary auditing works best, and the situations in which regulation is needed. There are at least four aspects that should be separated in the discussion of audit regulation. First, there is the demand for auditing, which is well established by literature and economic theory. There are many organizations or situations where auditors are already operating but where there is no forced imposition of an audit requirement. In those cases, there is a tendency that the audits will become compulsory, either because they add value to the economy or have positive externalities, or because lawmakers have incentives to impose this kind of regulation.

Second, there is the issue of who should conduct audits and under what conditions. These issues are often discussed under the general framework of competence and independence; that is, what is the best way to ensure that an auditor possesses adequate expertise to conduct an audit and to remain professionally skeptical about a client so as to not yield to pressure from various parties to reach specific conclusions. Regulations related to the education, training, and licensing of auditors are aimed at this problem, as are regulations that constrain the economic and personal links between a client and the auditor. Whether those regulations have the expected effect can be contentious. For example, there are numerous studies reporting conflicting conclusions about the effect of the requirement for 150 credit hours of university education in the United States (Allen and Woodland, 2006; Gramling and Rosman, 2009; Allen and Woodland, 2010; Woodland and Allen, 2012; Gramling and Rosman, 2013)

Third, there is the manner in which auditing is actually delivered. Do auditors do enough work? Can their procedures be improved? It is here where some regulation and standard setting may be beneficial, since neither clients nor stakeholders are in a position to evaluate whether an auditor's work is appropriate and comprehensive. Finally, and fourth, there is a strong concern about how to evaluate audit quality after the audit is completed. Regulations related to peer review and inspections are directed to this challenge. The question of whether they are sufficient is worth examining.

I Review and discussion

Auditing reduces the risk of a financial report being materially misstated. Auditing does not directly prevent financial losses, but it can ensure that information is more reliable, and that decisions are less likely to be made based on misleading information. Thus, auditing can be valuable to the users of financial reports, and when it is, it will also be of value to a company, its directors and managers, and outsiders such as investors and creditors.

More detailed explanations of the value of an audit to the company reporting are based on economic models: auditing as a way of signaling better quality financial reporting; auditing as a way to provide voluntary monitoring and bonding; auditing as a means of insurance for losses; auditing as a way to help managers to provide organizational control; auditing as a means of confirming the information in earlier announcements; and auditing as part of an overall risk management strategy.

There are competing explanations for why auditing is compulsory. Public interest models see compulsory auditing as a way to protect the interests of those stakeholders who cannot otherwise obtain auditing. Public choice models emphasize the interests of the legislators, perhaps in showing that they have taken some action during a crisis, and to deflect blame. As the preceding parts of this book show, auditing is complicated. Many of the explanations for auditing are counter-intuitive: it is in the manager's interest to arrange for auditing, so that it is not entirely necessary for it to be imposed by regulators. All the same, unless there are regulations, the extent of auditing may not be optimal for some stakeholders, or for the economy as a whole. Regulation may be for the benefit of the economy and for stakeholders who cannot impose their own controls on the company – but it may also be for the benefit of the regulators.

This book provides an overview of major research findings in selected areas with the hope that stakeholders in the audit process will learn about what is known about auditing, and what is possible from research. For academics, I hope to instigate more valuable research in the future. Auditing offers a challenging and vibrant domain for research. While large breakthroughs in audit research are rare, as noted by Trotman (2014), the contribution of researchers to knowledge and practice can be enhanced by a concentration on central themes and by incrementally building on previous research.

What is the future of auditing? Some observers see it as being currently at its peak, from which it will descend rapidly as technology develops in areas like big data and the blockchain. Others see it as having great potential to expand into wider and wider areas to provide valuable assurance over a wide range of issues, starting with sustainability and privacy. Auditing will always be a difficult task with conflicting demands and confused expectations. When people reflect on auditing in ten, 20, or 100 years' time, we can expect that it will still be in crisis, and many of the issues will be the same issues that concern us today.

References

Allen, A. C., and A. M. Woodland. 2006. The 150-Hour Requirement and the Number of CPA Exam Candidates, Pass Rates, and the Number Passing. *Issues in Accounting Education* 21 (3): 173–193.

———. 2010. Education Requirements, Audit Fees, and Audit Quality. *Auditing: A Journal of Practice & Theory* 29 (2): 1–25.

Anderson, U., and M. Christ. 2014. Internal Audit. In *The Routledge Companion to Auditing*, edited by D. C. Hay, W. R. Knechel, and M. Willekens, 230–239. Abingdon, UK: Routledge.

Audousset-Coulier, S., A. Jeny, and L. Jiang. 2016. The Validity of Auditor Industry Specialization Measures. *Auditing: A Journal of Practice & Theory* 35 (1): 139–161.

Bédard, J., and T. Compernolle. 2014. The Audit Committee. In *The Routledge Companion to Auditing*, edited by D. C. Hay, W. R. Knechel, and M. Willekens, 253–263. Abingdon, UK: Routledge.

Bedard, J. C., and L. Graham. 2014. Reporting on Internal Control. In *The Routledge Companion to Auditing*, edited by D. C. Hay, W. R. Knechel, and M. Willekens, 311–322. Abingdon, UK: Routldege.

Byrnes, P. E., A. Al-Awadhi, B. Gullvist, H. Brown-liburd, R. Teeter, J. D. Warren, and M. Vasarhelyi. 2012. Evolution of Auditing: From the Traditional Approach to the Future Audit. *AICPA White Paper*.

Cahan, S. F. 2014. Earnings Management and Auditing. In *The Routledge Companion to Auditing*, edited by D. C. Hay, W. R. Knechel, and M. Willekens, 119–129. Abingdon, UK: Routledge.

Carpenter, T. D., and A. A. Austin. 2014. Fraud and Auditors' Responsibility. In *The Routledge Companion to Auditing*, edited by D. C. Hay, W. R. Knechel, and M. Willekens, 107–118. Abingdon, UK: Routledge.

Carson, E. 2014. Globalization of Auditing. In *The Routledge Companion to Auditing*, edited by D. C. Hay, W. R. Knechel, and M. Willekens, 23–32. Abingdon, UK: Routledge.

Chandler, R., and J. R. Edwards. 1996. Recurring Issues in Auditing: Back to the Future? *Accounting, Auditing & Accountability Journal* 9 (2): 4–29.

Coram, P. 2014. Audit Reports. In *The Routledge Companion to Auditing*, edited by D. C. Hay, W. R. Knechel, and M. Willekens, 289–299. Abingdon, UK: Routledge.

DeAngelo, L. E. 1981. Auditor size and audit quality. *Journal of Accounting and Economics* 3 (3): 183–199.

Dey, R. M., A. Robin, and D. Tessoni. 2012, August. Advisory Services Rise Again at Large Audit Firms: Like a Phoenix, Revenues Reborn Amid Renewed Concerns. *The CPA Journal* 82: 58–67.

Doyle, J., W. Ge, and S. McVay. 2007. Determinants of weaknesses in internal control over financial reporting. *Journal of Accounting and Economics* 44 (1–2): 193–223.

Francis, J. R. 2004. What do We Know About Audit Quality? *British Accounting Review* 36 (4): 345–368.

Geiger, M. A. 2014. Going Concern. In *The Routledge Companion to Auditing*, edited by M. W. Hay, David C., W. Robert Knechel. Abingdon, UK: Routledge.

Gramling, L. J., and A. J. Rosman. 2009. The Ongoing Debate About the Impact of the 150-Hour Education Requirement on the Supply of Certified Public Accountants. *Issues in Accounting Education* 24 (4): 465–479.

———. 2013. The Ongoing Debate of and Direction for Future Research About the Impact of the 150-Hour Education Requirement on the Supply of Certified Public Accountants. *Issues in Accounting Education* 28 (3): 503–512.

Hay, D. C. 2018a. The Potential for Greater Use of Meta-Analysis in Archival Auditing Research. *Managerial Auditing Journal* 34 (1): 76–95. Accepted.

———. 2018b. Audit Fee Research on Issues Related to Ethics. *Current Issues in Auditing* 11 (2): A1–A22. ciia-51897.

Hay, D. C., W. R. Knechel, and M. Willekens. 2014. The Future of Auditing Research. In *The Routledge Companion to Auditing*, edited by D. C. Hay, W. R. Knechel, and M. Willekens, 351–357. Abingdon, UK: Routledge.

Hay, D. C., J. Stewart, and N. Botica Redmayne. 2017. The Role of Auditing in Corporate Governance in Australia and New Zealand: A Research Synthesis. *Australian Accounting Review* 27 (4): 457–479.

Holderness, D. K. 2014. Continuous Auditing. In *The Routledge Companion to Auditing*, edited by D. C. Hay, W. R. Knechel, and M. Willekens. Abingdon, UK: Routledge.

IAASB. 2013. *A Framework for Audit Quality: Discussion Paper*. New York, NY: IAASB.

———. 2014. *A Framework for Audit Quality*. New York, NY: IAASB.

Jeter, D. C. 2014. Auditor Industry Specialization. In *The Routledge Companion to Auditing*, edited by D. C. Hay, W. R. Knechel, and M. Willekens, 191–199. Abingdon, UK: Routledge.

Jones, H. 2018. UK to Consider Proposals to Curb Big Four Auditors: Industry Official. *Reuters*. www.reuters.com/article/britain-accounts-regulator/uk-to-consider-proposals-to-curb-big-four-auditors-industry-official-idUSL8N1VK30F

Khlif, H., and K. Chalmers. 2015. A Review of Meta-Analytic Research in Accounting. *Journal of Accounting Literature* 35: 1–27.

Knechel, W. R., G. V. Krishnan, M. Pevzner, L. B. Shefchik, and U. K. Velury. 2013. Audit Quality: Insights From the Academic Literature. *Auditing: A Journal of Practice & Theory* 32 (Supplement 1): 385–421.

Knechel, W. R., and L. B. Shefchik. 2014. Audit Quality. In *The Routledge Companion to Auditing*, edited by D. C. Hay, W. R. Knechel, and Willek, 130–147. Abingdon, UK: Routledge.

Kranacher, M., B. W. Morris, T. A. Pearson, and R. A. Riley. 2008. A Model Curriculum for Education in Fraud and Forensic Accounting. *Issues in Accounting Education* 23 (4): 505–519.

Langli, J. C., and T. Svanstrom. 2014. Audits of Private Companies. In *The Routledge Companion to Auditing*, edited by D. C. Hay, W. R. Knechel, and M. Willekens, 148–158. Abingdon, UK: Routledge.

Marriage, M. 2018. Watchdog Urges Audit Only Firms. *Financial Times*. http://link.gale-group.com/apps/doc/A531129230/AONE?u=learn&sid=AONE&xid=690c6338.

Maxwell, S. E., M. Y. Lau, and G. S. Howard. 2015. Is Psychology Suffering From a Replication Crisis? What Does "Failure to Replicate" Really Mean? *American Psychologist* 70 (6): 487–498.

Minutti-Meza, M. 2013. Does Auditor Industry Specialization Improve Audit Quality? *Journal of Accounting Research* 51 (4): 779–817.

Offermans, M., and A. Vanstraelen. 2014. Oversight and Inspection of Auditing. In *The Routledge Companion to Auditing*, edited by D. C. Hay, W. R. Knechel, and M. Willekens, 179–188. Abingdon, UK: Routledge.

Open Science Collaboration. 2015. Estimating the Reproducibility of Psychological Science. *Science* 349 (6251): aac4716–aac4716.

Porter, B. 2014. The Audit Expectation Gap: A Persistent But Changing Phenomenon. In *The Routledge Companion to Auditing*, edited by D. C. Hay, W. R. Knechel, and M. Willekens, 43–53. Abingdon, UK: Routledge.

Sharma, D. S. 2014. Non-Audit Services and Auditor Independence. In *The Routledge Companion to Auditing*, edited by D. C. Hay, W. R. Knechel, and M. Willekens, 67–88. Abingdon, UK: Routledge.

Shaub, M. K., and R. L. Braun. 2014. Auditing Ethics. In *The Routledge Companion to Auditing*, edited by D. C. Hay, W. R. Knechel, and M. Willekens, 264–275. Abingdon, UK: Routledge.

Simnett, R. 2014. Assurance of Environment, Social and Sustainability Information. In *The Routledge Companion to Auditing*, edited by D. C. Hay, W. R. Knechel, and M. Willekens, 325–337. Abingdon, UK: Routldege.

Stewart, J. 2014. Editorial: A Retrospective on the International Journal of Auditing, and a Call for Collaborative Research Involving Less Developed Regions. *International Journal of Auditing* 18 (3): 171–171.

Susskind, R., and D. Susskind. 2015. *The Future of the Professions*. Ebook. Oxford, UK: Oxford University Press.

Trotman, K. T. 2014. Judgment and Decision Making. In *The Routledge Companion to Auditing*, edited by D. C. Hay, W. R. Knechel, and M. Willekens, 200–218. Abingdon, UK: Routledge.

United States Treasury. 2008. Final Report of the Advisory Committee on the Auditing Profession to the U.S. Department of the Treasury. *Advisory Committee on the Audit Profession*. Washington, DC: United States Treasury.

Woodland, A. M., and A. C. Allen. 2012. Response to "The Ongoing Debate About the Impact of the 150-Hour Education Requirement on the Supply of Certified Public Accountants". *Issues in Accounting Education* 27 (4): 1045–1057.

Index

Abdel-khalik, A. R. 8, 12
accounting trends 27–32
agency (or monitoring) explanation for
    value of auditing 4–6, 12
assurance, new forms of 57–58
auditing: economic benefits of 1;
    general definition of 1; global
    or national 34–36; historical
    development of 17–19; importance
    of 1, 15–17; in less-developed
    countries 16; privacy 17, 30; as
    public good 14; public sector 16–17;
    quality control 28–29; regulation of
    13–15, 30–31, 36; *see also* future of
    auditing; research; value of auditing
audit markets 53–54
audit quality research 50–51
audit society 11
Austin, A. A. 58
automation 32–34

Baber, W. R. 12
Baker, C. R. 10, 15
Ball, R. 9–10, 15
Banker, R. D. 16
Baskerville, R. F. 40
Bédard, J. C. 9, 10, 15, 54, 55
big data 29
Braun, R. L. 57
Brown, P. 9
Bush, G. W. 15

Cameron, D. 39
Carpenter, T. D. 58
climate change 26–27
coercive isomorphism 10

Compernolle, T. 9, 54, 55
confirmation hypothesis 9–10
Cooper, W. W. 16
Cordery, C. J. 16
corporate governance: explanation for
    value of auditing 8–9, 12; research
    on auditing and 54–55
corporate social responsibility (CSR) 17
cross-border regulation 53–54
crypto-currencies 32

digital money 32

economic theory of regulation 13–14
Eierle, B. 35
ethics, auditing 57
Evans, J. H. 12
evidence-based auditing standards
    36–38
expectation gap 28, 57

Facebook 29
Fama, E. F. 40
FEE (the Fédération des
    Expertscomptables) Européens 27
financial statements 19n4
Firth, M. 12
Forbes Insights for the Global Public
    Policy Committee 27
Francis, J. R. 35, 36
fraud research 58–59
future of auditing: evidence-based
    auditing standards and 36–38; global
    or national auditing and 34–36;
    global trends in 25–27; information
    technology and automation and

32–34; partnership model in 39–41; predictions about 41–43; relevant audits for wide range of stakeholders in 38–39; trends in accounting and 27–32; *see also* auditing

global or national auditing 34–36
global trends in future of auditing 25–27
Google 29, 30
governance and auditing 54–55
Graham, L. 54

Hartlieb, S. 35
Hay, D. C. 12, 16, 35, 40
He, S. 12
hindsight bias 28
historical development of auditing 17–19
Hoang, H. 30
Holderness, D. K. 58

ICAEW "Future of Audit" project 34
importance of auditing 1, 15–17
independence, auditor 51–52
information (or signaling) explanation for value of auditing 6, 12
information technology and automation 32–34
innovative settings 56–57
institutional theory 10
insurance (or "deep pockets") explanation for value of auditing 7, 12
integrated reporting (IR) 29
International Auditing and Assurance Board (IAASB) 31, 37, 51
International Ethics Standards Board for Accountants (IESBA) 37
International Federation of Accountants (IFAC) 33
International Federation of Independent Audit Regulators (IFIAR) 36

Jayaraman, S. 9
Jensen, M. C. 40
Jeter, D. C. 53
Journal of Accounting and Economics 37
judgment research 59

Knechel, W. R. 8–9, 30, 50, 51
Krishnan, G. V. 51

Langli, J. C. 56
legitimacy theory 10

Maltby, J. 18
management control explanation for value of auditing 7–8, 12
Mansi, S. A. 12
mimetic isomorphism 10

neo-institutional theory 10
Niemi, L. 35
Nikkinen, J. 35
normative isomorphism 10

Offermans, M. 52
Ojala, H. 35

Pacini, C. 13
partnership model of auditing 39–41
Patton, J. M. 12
Pevzner, M. 51
Porter, B. 28
Potter, G. 16
Power, M. 11
Prat dit Hauret, C. 10, 15
predictions about future of auditing 41–43
price protection 5
privacy auditing 17, 30
Public Company Accounting Oversight Board (PCAOB) 34
public good, auditing as 14
public sector auditing 16–17

quality control audits 28–29

Rajan, R. G. 14
regulation of auditing 13–15, 30–31, 36; research on 52–53; *see also* auditing
relevant audits for various stakeholders 38–39
replications of research studies 56
research: auditing in private companies and other settings 55–56; audit markets 53–54; auditor independence 51–52; audit quality 50–51; governance and auditing 54–55; regulation and auditing 52–53; review and discussion of 60–61; under-researched areas of

auditing 56–59; unresolved issues requiring further 59–60

Sahlström, P. 35
Sarbanes-Oxley Act 10, 15
Schelleman, C. 38
Sharma, D. S. 51–52
Shaub, M. K. 57
Shefchik, L. B. 50, 51
Shivakumar, L. 9
Shore, C. 11
Simnett, R. 30, 58
specific audits 38–39
Srinidhi, B. N. 12
stakeholder theory 10
Susskind, D. 33–34
Susskind, R. 33–34
Svanstrom, T. 56

technology and automation 32–34
Thompson, P. 33
Trotman, K. T. 59, 61

value of auditing 2, 3–4; agency (or monitoring) explanation 4–6, 12; confirmation hypothesis explanation 9–10; corporate governance explanation 8–9, 12; evidence about explanations for 11–13; explanations for 4–11; information (or signaling) explanation 6, 12; insurance (or "deep pockets") explanation 7, 12; management control explanation 7–8, 12; other explanations for 10–11; *see also* auditing
Vanstraelen, A. 38, 52
Velury, U. K. 51

Watts, R. L. 15, 17–18
Willekens, M. 3, 8–9
World Bank 14, 35, 56
Wright, S. 11

Zhou, S. 30
Zimmerman, J. L. 12, 15, 17–18
Zingales, L. 14